MW00644258

the stories that make us

a memoir transforming shame into power

Lauren Eckhardt

burning soul press

contents

The Stories That Make Us
a memoir transforming shame into power

by
Lauren Eckhardt

Special Edition Cover: Dee Dee Books
Dust Jacket & Paperback Cover: Creative Paramita

eBook ISBN: 978-1-950476-83-1
Paperback ISBN: 978-1-950476-82-4
Hardcover ISBN: 978-1-950476-81-7

Copyright © 2023 Lauren Eckhardt

This memoir is a personal account of my life as I recall it. The memories and perspectives shared within these pages are mine alone and may not accurately represent the objective facts or the experiences of others involved. The events and conversations have been recounted to the best of my ability, but given the nature of memory, some details may not be precise.

The names of some individuals have been excluded to protect their privacy. Any resemblance to other persons, living or dead, or to actual events or locales is entirely coincidental.

This work is copyrighted. No part of this publication may be reproduced, distributed, or transmitted in any form or by any means, including photocopying, recording, or other electronic or mechanical methods, without the prior written permission of the author, except in the case of brief quotations embodied in critical reviews and certain other noncommercial uses permitted by copyright law.

For permission requests, please contact Lauren Eckhardt.

For Easton & Camden
and for every single person who needs to share their story.

important, not worthless

My story isn't important enough.
There isn't a big enough event that took place.
I didn't have a lot of trauma.
I'm not a celebrity.
I have to do more and be more before I can write anything people would care to read.
I'm going to be embarrassing my entire family if I share this.
I'm going to hurt my family/my friends/people if I share this.
No one cares about what I have to say.
This is incredibly shameful to admit, and I don't think I can write it down for complete strangers to judge.

EVERYTHING ABOVE IS WHAT I HEAR CLIENTS SAY WHEN they come to me, expressing interest in hiring me to help them write their life story so it can be captured in a book. There are variations of each one, but these are the most popular lines I hear time and again.

They're also the exact fears that have held me back from sharing my own story.

Yet when I hear them coming out of someone else's mouth, I can see how wrong it sounds to let all these fears block them from such an important act. So I patiently listen to all the reasons they've told themselves for why sharing their story isn't important. Then I gently remind them of the reason *why* they felt the nudge to share in the first place.

I tell them, "There's a greater reason for sharing your story that you can't fully see yet, but you can *feel* it, which is why you thought about it in the first place. Your life is important. It's meaningful. Look at what you've achieved, at what you've learned, at how you've grown. Look at your resilience, the way you've overcome obstacles of all shapes and sizes, the way you've thrived under insane pressure and expectations and hardships and more. Look at what you've come to learn and realize about yourself and the world. Your experience here is absolutely worth sharing! There are so many people who need to hear this!"

I believe that to be true at the core of my being for every single person I've coached and for every single person I have yet to meet.

But yet, I still wasn't sharing my story because I didn't feel like people would care. I didn't feel like it mattered.

I still had a lot of inner work to do.

Adding to the list of fears above, one of my personal fears is hearing, "That's not what happened. Your memory is off." I find it funny that I've allowed that to stand in my way. Excuses driven by fear reveal parts of ourselves that are yet to be healed and this one shows how much I'm still operating by this people-pleasing, never-want-to-be-wrong mode that I've been fighting throughout the years. Disagreements with my family about past events has made me doubt not only my memory, but what I learned and now know from those memories. But it's not enough to stay quiet. Because regardless if someone remembers something differently than I do, my memories are mine and have shaped me. They are inside me, impacting my belief system, my reactions, my actions, my views, my perspectives, my emotions.

Memory is a funny thing. It's faulty and imperfect, but our emotions and how these events made us feel in the moment stay with us forever. They became stories I've held on to—affecting me every minute of every day, whether I recognize it or not. These memories are a flowing undercurrent, until I address them head on and understand them for what they are.

Over the years of working as a book coach and ghostwriter in the nonfiction field, I've come to see the power of writing a memoir: releasing the stories that have held us captive for too long; seeing them for what they truly are; choosing whether to keep them as part of our identity, or let them go. We start to realize that these stories don't have to play an active role in our lives today if we don't want them to, because, ultimately, we have the power to choose.

The thing is, when people share their stories, it empowers others to do the same. They realize they're not alone and that other people are facing similar challenges or experiences. We don't truly connect with others until we see past all the surface-level stuff. The only way to go deep, is to reveal a genuine part of who we are and create the opportunity for someone else to do the same. When we connect over things, big and small, we rise. Together, we step into our most authentic selves and discover our inner power. Only then do we know how we can work with each other, and when we work with each other, we can then make a difference in shaping this world for the better.

I've come to realize that part of my greater purpose is to help people write their life stories to feel seen and heard for who they truly are as their most authentic and vulnerable self. But above all, to truly connect with each other on the soul level that we were designed to be connected at. I lean toward capturing stories in books because of the staying power of books and their ability to inspire, empower, and help many others while being passed down from one set of hands to another.

But whether people choose to write it in a book or not, I believe they should always take the time to honor the importance of their life by writing it and documenting it. First for them, then for their family, and finally, if they so choose, to share it with the world.

So, to help lead this mission, I knew it was time to share my story. And in helping people uncover their own courage, I found my own.

I now acknowledge that my story is important, too. My words, steps, and actions all matter here. I'm leaving a legacy every day I'm alive. It's up to me to capture it, though. There may be paper trails when I'm gone, but the full story as told from my perspective, that's something only I can do.

I have two boys, Easton (eight) and Camden (five). I started writing my memoir when they were six and three. They are my *why* behind everything I do. They represent the future. They are my beacons of hope that I can somewhat shape the future to be as good as the kids I raise. I hope to God they are inspired by this book, rather than hiding under the covers someday in embarrassment. But... vulnerability and visibility can go hand in hand, and hopefully they see that their mom is no longer afraid to be who God made her to be and the journey she's been on to get here.

So, here I am, world.

The good, the bad, the light, the dark—all of it is about to be told. In honor of complete transparency and transformation, I'm going to share the stories that I allowed to shape me. It's the humiliating moments that scare me the most because those stories reveal how much I didn't see my worth and how I gave my power over to other people over and over for most of my life. Layered deeply throughout these stories is the feeling of shame. Shame holds us all back. When we're held back, we're hindered in reaching our God-given purpose in this world. We're held back from living freely. We're stuck living in a place of regrets as our inner light dims and fades because we're not accepting who we are and how we've gotten to where we are today. And that shame is something that held me back—until now.

In healing and hindsight, when I reflect back on my life, I see a girl who once had constant chaos within her, desperate to be anyone other than herself—who wanted love, but didn't know how to receive it. In trying to make everyone else happy, she lost herself. She made terrible decisions, put herself in bad situations, and had to experience things several times before finally learning lessons she should have known all along.

I used to be ashamed of that girl. I've decided I can't do that to myself any longer.

I was so focused on other people's perceptions and opinions of me. I constantly adjusted and changed myself to satisfy unspoken expectations, so much so that I never looked inward to see how I truly felt. It took me a while to get to know who I really am as a result.

Honestly, one of the yet-unsaid fears that quickens my heart rate is that people will see me differently. I worry people I love will only see my most shameful stories, and hold me to some of the worst in-the-moment decisions I made. I fear they will still view me with the same dark lens I've viewed myself in for far too long, not willing to accept or see that I'm different now because of the grace and power of God.

It's the same thing I tell my clients, though: You're going to have people who read your story and hang on to who you once were because it makes them feel better to see you that way. Don't let that diminish from the real people who see how you're different because of the unique journey you went on and how you've changed. People you don't know will deeply appreciate and relate to your story—especially the hardest-to-tell pieces. If you know your story needs to be told, you need to stay focused on how it makes *you* feel to release the stories and how it feels to connect deeply with others *because* you shared your story.

When we feel convicted to share our stories, it's not our job to determine how the reader will respond or how the reader will see us; but it is our job to use those stories to bring awareness. In bringing awareness to these pieces of ourselves that have been pushed down, shoved away, and neglected for too long, we can heal. It's a chance to get to see the real us through a new lens and bring a new narrative to our present and future, while helping others heal as well.

Maybe people will think I'm weird after reading my life story.

Maybe they won't want to be friends. Maybe they'll bash me in reviews and on social media.

But maybe a few people will feel less weird and less alone... and this book is for them.

This book is also for those who have been thinking about writing a memoir, or sharing their life story in some way, but they're terrified. They don't know where to start or what to share or not share. For me, I want to unveil it all, knowing how uncomfortable it's going to be for me, and perhaps for the reader at times as well. But I want to wade through the discomfort in order to turn it into power, to turn it into good. I'm re-writing the narratives that have held me back for far too long so my future and the future of my kids look differently.

And I pray for equal boldness for others as they set out on their path and decide what they share.

Besides, if we knew that what we're writing is going to be life-changing for at least one person in this world, wouldn't we write it no matter what?

So, here's my story... all for the one person who needs it the most.

valued, not invisible

GROWING UP IN THE BOONDOCKS OF SOUTHERN Missouri meant being surrounded by dirt roads, playing in mud holes or with toilet paper (or both at the same time), heroically saving Bluebird eggs that would drop from nests, and weaving in and out of houses with large yards protected by electric fences, where hogs in the backyard was normal. It also meant daring other neighborhood kids to touch random plants that would numb our fingers, bouncing on a trampoline protected by a scary 150-pound St. Bernard, and hiding from tornadoes in the bathtub with a mattress pulled over our heads.

Bernie, Missouri, located right on the bootheel of the state, is where I spent the most formative years of my life. A simple town with no stoplight and no hospital, but a large piece of community playground equipment shaped like a red, white, and blue rocket that seemed like a straight shot out of there—except its extreme height coupled with my fear of falling kept me closer to the ground.

I didn't appreciate the beauty of being raised in a small town for what it was. Now I find myself wishing for the same simplicity today. Where things weren't so accessible so we had to make do with what we had and be challenged to use our imaginations instead.

There were seemingly less limitations during that time. It felt like the entire world was our place to explore. We came and went as freely as we wanted, very few adults ever in our presence. I don't remember my parents telling us what we could or could not do, although surely they did. It seemed there was a lot of space to figure things out because the adults were busy figuring things out and just surviving.

I grew up with two older brothers, Garrett and Isaac. Both my parents worked full time, so they weren't around often. My dad traveled as a Conductor for the railroad and was hardly in town at all. He had his own trailer he lived in wherever he was working at the time. Usually, he'd only come home for a day and a half on the weekends before he set out again.

When he would be home, he seemed to always have a migraine, his head wrapped up with my mom's pantyhose to alleviate the pressure. When Dad had a migraine, it was crucial to stay as quiet as possible. So outside we continued to play. My brothers went off with their friends and I tried to keep up, but I was the little sister. One of my favorite places to go was a haven in the form of a giant shrub that I made into my own mini treehouse—a *shrubhouse*, if you will, where I learned that the safest place to be was where I wasn't bothering anyone else. Smaller I withdrew, creating the life-shaping story that it was best if I didn't take up any room or make much noise.

I would hide in my shrubhouse for hours, surrounded by greenery and sticks. No one else ever entered; I had complete dominion. I decorated it with random trinkets, colorful strings, and scraps of paper, and left notes for mysterious people I imagined would come across my scribbles. In fact, I left notes in many places (including behind dressers and buried in the ground), as though already believing in the power of words: their staying power; their ability to connect two people together; their ability to represent our time and make our memory known.

For many years, I held a belief that I was wearing an invisibility cloak, like when every other raised hand was getting called on in class other than mine. Or when I would be the last one chosen for games like Red Rover. Or even as an adult, I believed I had the most forgettable face; it would seem I'd meet people one day, and they'd forget me the next.

I would do the darnest things to try to get attention, thinking that maybe someday, someone would think I'm cool. Like naptime at my babysitter's when surrounded by other kids, I'd actually try to sleep with my legs over my head as though that would set me apart. Needless to say, I didn't actually nap in that position, but man I thought I was standing out. I imagined people watching me wishing they could be like that, too.

I always wanted to believe people were watching me and thinking something good about me. I'd often pretend I was performing my life when I was in school or in public, rather than living it, but when I'd turn my head, no one was actually looking.

What's funny is that the moment someone *did* bring their attention to me, I would shrink back, become mute, and want to hide. I was just as prone to deflect attention as much as I craved it at the same time. A fear dominated my thoughts for as long as I could remember that being seen put me at risk of my safety being stripped away. It seemed if I was *seen*, I was at risk of judgment, confirmation that I was unworthy, or a violation of my body. Unfortunately, that fear seemed to manifest experiences throughout my life that validated the belief.

A part of me is desperate to believe that in those early days of life I knew how to truly be *me*. Me without a filter or mask or a fear of disappointing people influencing my every move. Playing, laughing, creating... surely there has to be *some* point in life when I knew how to be exactly me.

Pictures and videos jog my memory, otherwise, I wouldn't have many memories from childhood. I have always questioned why I've blocked so much out. I know I was violated early in life, but no matter the attempts at recall, my body desperately keeps the details of that memory blocked out. As an adult, I've tried psychotherapy techniques, but my inner voice pleaded with me, "No, no, no, don't go there! Don't uncover it!" So I continued to push it away. No matter how hazy, the past still carries weight and influences my present and the future. I can feel this in every interaction I have, especially in relation to intimacy (both sexual and non-sexual). My emotional and reflexive response runs deeper than what's just happening in that moment.

I've noticed the limited memories I do have seem to be dressed in shame or sadness. Maybe that's why I escaped the version of me I knew at one point; I was ashamed of her.

The one thing I know how to do above all else is *feel*, and deeply, at that. I've been a queen of that my entire life—except usually it's related to feeling not-so-happy things. I've been working hard over the past five years to try to correct this trend; to ensure that the happiest of moments and gratitude flood my mind first. Lord knows that as a mom, I don't want my kids to only think of the negative times in their lives, especially when I try so hard to fill every single day of theirs with love. So I'm sure my parents won't like knowing that most of my memories from the first part of my life are associated with pain.

Sometimes I wish I had a video of my life so I could rewind it and pay attention to the most joyful moments that somehow I let wash away. Instead, the videos I do have, I just see the underlying chaos going through the little girl on camera. The one who felt comfortable only when alone.

When I first heard the term "wallflower," I felt seen, ironically enough. The push and pull between the deep desire of wanting to be understood and not wanting to be too vulnerable was a constant battle. When I wasn't being acknowledged, I wished desperately that someone would notice me. I wanted to know what it was like to be recognized, to be loved, to be accepted. I wanted to feel like I was worthy of it.

I wanted love and acceptance from my family, but I wasn't getting it in the way I needed. We all love and receive love differently. When my dad returned from his work trips, he'd give me a little toy, or more often a box of animal crackers. For him, love came in the form of a gift to make up for his absence. I wanted explicit words of affection and conversations.

I used to brag that my dad and I would say "I hate you" more than we ever said we loved each other. We were comfortably sarcastic with each other, a communication style I regularly exercised because of his influence. That sarcasm became a defense mechanism, though. To this day, I have to avoid using it when I feel myself starting to crave the love and attention of someone else. Because ultimately, it keeps people at arm's length.

It took me a good four decades to get comfortable enough to tell people that I love them, even my own family. Now we say it fairly regularly but my discomfort is an automatic response I'm still trying to break.

Everything in my life comes back to words. Words have always been important to me. Whether reading them in books, struggling to speak what's in my mind, spending hours writing them on paper... words have defined my heart, my mind, my life. I would argue that's true for most people when we stop and think about it. Words carry immense value from the time we enter the world, which is why we anticipate what word our kids will say as their first word. For me, the value of actions (whether in the form of a gift or an act of service) comes secondary, and only holds significance when they reinforce the words that were said.

Back then, more so than today where "conscious parenting" is a trendy term, most parents were just doing the best they could. As long as it was better than how *they* were parented, they considered it a win. It wasn't that I was actually invisible to my parents when I hid away in makeshift treehouses or escaped into fantasy worlds. They were just doing the best they could to survive and provide for us, while navigating life themselves. But as kids, we are inescapably molded by each interaction, no matter the intention.

It's strange to me that I don't have many day-to-day memories that involve my parents. I'm not sure how it's possible to spend that much time with someone and not retain any of it. The memories I do have with my parents mostly surround experiences; a handful of trips to California to see extended family as well as going to Dolly-wood and Gatlinburg. Or when I was a tween and my mom spent time taking me on little field trips throughout Central and Southern Illinois to feed into my love for learning, such as to the Amish country or Cahokia Mounds State Park.

It makes me wonder what sort of memories my own children will have of me, and if these special little daily moments that mean so much to me may not last for them. I try so hard to do better than my parents did for me, by telling them how much I love them and giving them hugs and kisses daily, and taking them places and doing things together—trying every technique possible to flex to their individual love languages. But how can I know what's sticking, or what sort of less-than-ideal moments are wiping them away?

No matter what they remember, what doesn't change is how valued they are. I see them even when they may not think I'm watching, and they're constantly on my mind even when they may not know it. I replay looks they give me, words they say, and things they do for days after. I get more excited to see their reaction to the things we do than the experiences themselves. I flip through pictures on my phone of them every night, minutes after I just put them to bed, as though I've been without them for weeks.

The perspective parenthood has given me has made me realize that even the times I tend to believe I'm invisible or am not being recognized in the way I want, there's actually someone's mind I'm probably on. There is someone who is thinking of each of us. I've had to go back and tell that little girl that in all the times she thought she was insignificant, she was making a difference in the lives of those who love her. Her presence mattered, even when she didn't know it.

introspective, not irritating

THERE'S A HOME VIDEO WE HAVE ON ONE OF THOSE OLD 8mm recorders of me around six years old. I'm hitting a punching balloon and singing in a thick, Southern accent that I can barely understand, "Pump, pump a jam." My light blond hair flaps in my face and the wind, as the cameraman tries to avoid me.

I've seen this home video maybe twice but there's something that struck me about it: it makes me feel very, very, *very* uncomfortable.

This little girl, although obnoxious, was clearly seeking attention, yet the adult operating the camera still moves above her head —trying to focus on anything but her. I'm irritated when watching it, irritated by the way it replays in my mind, and I can only assume everyone else was as irritated by me as it felt.

I think of this video often, and strangely, use it as my image of myself, the way I identify, even throughout my thirties. It's all I can see when I look in the mirror or speak or try to exist among other people. I'm still that annoying little girl who no one wants to see or hear. It's the story that has stuck around the longest and shown up the most.

When I look back at pictures of my childhood, there are very few in which I don't look incredibly awkward in my own skin.

Where I don't look uncomfortable having a camera pointed in my direction. Where I don't try to mirror the people next to me and fail.

Maybe it's because somewhere deep down, I can remember what I felt like in those moments. So, when I see the pictures, it's obvious, as though my feelings are written on every inch of my body.

I struggled to express these feelings out loud, so I wrote them down on paper. The pages became my safety when the world around me felt unstable, when I didn't fit in, when it felt like the love I craved was nowhere to be found. I had to create a new story instead.

When I was a little girl, adults—many who were strangers—would sit next to me and tell me their life stories. The times I have heard, "I've never told anyone this before," or "I can't believe I just shared that," are mind-blowing. I didn't understand it when I was young, but intuitively I knew to stay quiet and to listen because it was clear they needed to be heard.

I was a designated priest without the outfit or the qualifications. As I got older, I seemed to become a confessional booth for all ages, not just adults. I liked being a safe space where people felt comfortable talking about themselves, but I was fairly certain that most people wanted me around just because I would listen to them.

After a while, it became exasperating. I expected to be heard in exchange for listening, but very few people wanted to listen to me without talking over me. At first, these interactions reinforced my belief that I'm not important enough to be heard and that I'm annoying when I speak. But over time, I realized I have a deep and sincere interest in how people become who they are for a reason. I know how important it is to show someone, even for a brief moment, that they matter and they're heard.

Listening more than speaking made it more difficult to know how to speak about myself. I only came out of my shell when it was to be there for somebody else—to be who and what they needed. To this day, I can ask someone a billion questions about who they are with pure curiosity, but once they want to know about me, I struggle to share without turning the question back to them as quickly as possible.

There was a six-year and eight-year gap between me and my older brothers, which made me feel like not only the youngest child and only girl, but also another first-born. Maybe that's partly why every personality assessment I take ends up with middle-of-the-road results. I can be this and that, a little bit of everything. It allows me to adapt and understand many people's perspectives, which has come in handy as I help people write their life stories. But it also makes me feel like no one, outside of less than a handful of people in my life, can really understand all the layers, depth, and the full circumference of how I feel and think.

Others try to peg it, but there's always so much more. When people believed they knew who I was, I just nodded and silently thought, *But you don't because you haven't dug deeper than what you assume about me.* Instead of trying to show them, I would shrink further within myself. I allowed their expectations to shape me into someone simpler, who may be understood. I prioritized validating their beliefs about me. This was the start of my people-pleasing tendencies.

As a result, I dove deeper into writing because it was the one time I could "speak" and be heard, to be able to express myself fully without the people-pleaser filter. In conversation, it felt like I was on a timer with pressure to say the right thing. *How quickly can I speak before somebody interrupts what I'm saying? How quickly can I speak before someone is bored with what I'm saying? How quickly can I speak before it becomes clear that I didn't say what they wanted me to say?* With writing, I had the time and space to get my thoughts out. It's how I best process what's going on in my mind and heart.

When I was nine years old, I opened up a brand-new spiral-bound notebook, took out a pencil, and started writing a collection of essays. These essays captured my thoughts on a variety of topics from racism to divorce to the criminal system to the state of affairs in this world and more. Apparently, it was my first nonfiction book in the making. It's hard to believe that I could comprehend the depth of those topics at such a young age. At the time, it felt important to capture my thoughts as though I had rock-solid views that could never waiver. I called the collection "One Burning Soul," which unexpectedly played a significant role later when starting a business that would change my life.

Around the time I wrote that collection, I had a vision. This vision was of a person stuck in a glass box, pounding on the walls, screaming for help, yet people just walked by, unable to see or hear the person in the glass box. It haunted me. I later used this image as a scene in my first book, *The Remedy Files: Illusion*, because I couldn't shake it, even decades later.

What I didn't realize at the time, was that vision was a call to break out of my own glass box, and to help others free themselves as well. It was a call to make every single human being see how important they are. It was a calling on my life. Unfortunately, it took many years for me to see it for what it was. Now, the glass box vision and the "Burning Soul" collection have shapeshifted to promote hope and reform more than represent despair and anguish.

It amazes me how clear I was on my future as a child without realizing how clear I actually was.

While I found solace in my little shrubhouse all alone, writing notes for random people to find someday, I also developed a deep appreciation of trees. I became fascinated with roots and how some are ugly and some are beautiful, but they're all unique strands that contribute equally to the growth of the tree itself. I admired the seasons trees go through, the beauty of old leaves dropping away, the bareness as they wait to grow new ones, and their strength through all conditions and circumstances. I realized trees are a reflection of us—and their story is a reflection of the universal human story. Trees taught me to look past what we can see on the outside and to truly lean in and understand the complexities that form each of us.

To this day, I can still sit and stare at a tree for hours. I swear I can hear them talking. They bring me peace to be in their presence.

I have a certain tree scene that I scribble often on random pieces of paper. A big oak tree, half of a sun, and a few birds flying around. I drew my first one in second grade, and it's a mindless habit that comforts me in a strange way. Now my kids will draw the same scene because they've seen me do it so often.

While I may have felt like those periods of isolation were a rejection of not fitting in anywhere else, what I see now is if I didn't have those periods of isolation, I wouldn't have discovered what makes me tick on such a deep level: trees, creativity, words, and stories. Ironically, they were the same things God used to reflect my true purpose in the moments I questioned it the most. They're also the same things helping me build the legacy I want to leave in this world.

I'm sure I hadn't even heard of the word "legacy" by then, let alone knew what it meant, how it would shape me today, and influence everything I do. All I knew is that despite being alone regularly, I wanted to be known but didn't know how to allow myself to be known. My fear of being irritating to others kept me withdrawn and introspective, molding to what I assumed other people wanted from me instead. But all the years of being painfully aware of how I was falling short of keeping up with other people, made me also be able to unearth who I truly am when I was ready to embrace my fullest expression.

Nothing during this time was wasted, and it's really cool to see that in all the times I thought I was irritating and invisible, I was actually being pointed to all the things that make me, *me*.

curious, not dirty

WHEN I WAS FOUR YEARS OLD, I SPENT MOST OF MY DAYS at my babysitter's house. I played in the sandbox, ate wafer cookies, created Lite Brite works of art, pulled peaches off the tree only to be revolted by the fuzziness, cut open apples in search of worms, and received lessons in Miss Kathryn's basement that was set up like a schoolhouse. She was a former school teacher turned daycare provider. To this day, I can still see the cardboard pictures of every letter in the alphabet taped to the concrete wall. A is for Apple. B is for Bear. C is for Cat. D is for Doll. I credit my love for learning in part to her. She taught me how to read early which lit my fire for books at a young age.

Miss Kathryn seemed to be the only adult around while wrangling a house full of kids. I have one vague memory of her husband, but I don't recall if he was actually ever around. Kids ran wild, free to roam her house and yard for most of the day. But it worked; I don't think she lost any of us in all that time.

I had a massive crush on two boys, Waylon and Matt. As kids do, I debated which one I would marry someday. One had bleach blonde hair and blue eyes and a big, toothy smile. The other had brown hair, brown eyes, and a mischievous grin that melted me. They were total opposites of each other, so how was I to choose? A pattern was starting that hasn't ended to this day, where suddenly two potential love interests show up at the same time. And just like at daycare, they are opposites, so I have to figure out which one is better for me. Ironically, both almost-relationships usually end at the same time, so I end up alone again. That's a pattern that needs to be squashed.

There were also other girls at Miss Kathryn's house who I wondered if Waylon and Matt would like more. So, I had to step up and win them over. For some reason, I assumed the only way to do so was to be naked with them.

Miss Kathryn was upstairs making lunch while we played in the basement. I strategically positioned two playhouses together, and draped a blanket over the top of them so we could lay under the blanket between the playhouses. I invited Matt first (Waylon was next) and asked him to remove his shirt. Then I removed mine. I told Matt to lay on top of me. I had such an intense desire to be chest-to-chest, and here we were.

It didn't take long for some kid to tattle on us. Miss Kathryn yanked the blanket off the houses, pulling me up by the arm. Before embarrassment washed over me, I remember first feeling disappointment that I didn't get to do it with Waylon. She ruined my plan.

She took me upstairs and I listened while Miss Kathryn called my mom from the other room, straining to hear what she was saying. My heart raced while I waited for my mom to pick me up, my stomach turning. Shame was sinking in, even if I didn't have a name for it.

I don't know if Miss Kathryn ever told my parents. I don't remember getting in trouble.

But it was my first memory surrounding physical intimacy of many throughout the years without fully understanding my actions. Like using the cabinet door of our living room side table or the arm of a desk chair in my room to rub myself on. Trying to make out with boys in tires on the playground. Letting boys I barely knew touch me or kiss me in private areas. All I knew was that something made me feel good for a moment when I didn't feel very good about myself. It was a temporary high.

I didn't know what I was doing or what it was called. Just that there was this yearning inside of me fueled by pure desire for connection that filled my body and my mind in time periods when I should have been having tea parties with my dolls instead.

I wish someone had explained why our body reacts in that way sometimes; why we suddenly want to do things that feel good even if they don't make sense. I wish they had lovingly asked me why I felt the desire to lay naked with those boys and why I felt like it was something I needed to do to get them to like me.

As kids, we are constantly asking, "Why?" We're seeking answers, trying to make sense of the world around us—it's our natural inclination. When we aren't guided to the right answers, we make up our own. When we're struggling to make sense of things, we fill in the gaps with our own ideas.

Adults are often quick to react to the things kids do without asking *why* to discover the source of a behavior. I wish an adult had told me that it's okay to be curious about those things, and talked through it with me to find out why I did it. The "playing house" incident was never turned into a learning opportunity and the memory has left behind a shadow of shame and embarrassment. I've always replayed this memory through a lens of sexual desire that kicked off the years of confusion and hurt to come instead of recognizing a girl who was just seeking connection. Somehow I had developed a story that "to get their attention and be loved, you have to give your body over to them." I so very much wish I could go back and correct that little girl's belief because it followed her for the next three decades. When our curiosity is not quenched with real answers, what results is an incessant desire to make sense of it by exploring until we can understand.

My brothers would put my Barbies in compromising positions, making loud and unnecessary noises, using the word "dirty." I'd watch, embarrassed by their actions, yet also curious about how it would feel to be doing those things with someone. I realized I had to be dirty too because I tried to do those exact things with Matt and Waylon.

It made me feel uncomfortable to play with Barbies; they were too at risk of exposure with their easily-removable clothes. What I saw of myself in the Barbies is what I hated most about them. As a result, I drifted to Ninja Turtles instead. They felt safe. They had tools and skills to defend themselves. Suddenly, I wanted to be surrounded by masculinity. I craved the same control they had, the ease at which they navigated the world, not ashamed about their bodies. My brothers would moon each other (and even the video camera when my dad had it out) like it was no big deal. I took off my shirt with Matt and was immediately in trouble. There were different expectations but no one was actually explaining why men could so freely expose themselves and girls could not. It was the start of feeling like I didn't want to be a girl, because it wasn't fair.

Since I was my parents' only girl after two boys, my mom went crazy dressing me in pink clothes and dresses. She put me in beauty pageants, like the Miss Bernie Pageant where I had a grumpy smile on my face the whole time and walked fast across the stage, like I couldn't wait to get off. It didn't take long for me to completely reject pink. I wanted no association with it. Pink was also the color of Barbie. Pink seemed weak, and for many years, it repulsed me. Pink seemed to be at risk of making someone too vulnerable and dirty all in one.

The word "dirty" kept hanging on me, like I couldn't free myself from its grip. Like when I came across porn for the first, but definitely not the last, time. Or the way I made my body available time and again to men in desperation to fill a void I refused to acknowledge. "Dirty" would trigger me decades later—it took me a while to be willing to use it again, even when my sons would have dirt all over their faces. I had to get to the core of what it was causing within me and why.

As much as I wish an adult did intervene and provide healthy guidance during that time, I can't help but also be glad that they didn't. Anything that resembles sexual curiosity makes the majority of us feel uncomfortable. Many times when we face something that makes us uncomfortable, we want to squash it. Slash it. Retreat from it. Burn it. As fast as possible.

If an adult knew just how much sexual curiosity was driving my mind on a daily basis, someone not properly equipped with how to handle it may have squashed my curiosity as a whole. They wouldn't have seen through the action to what was at the root, which was the curiosity itself. They may have infused even more shame into me instead.

I wouldn't be who I am today without that curiosity within me being so strong.

That curiosity throughout the years has brought me down so many rabbit holes, but it's also what has helped me find my purpose; it's what has helped me be as successful as I am today as a book coach and ghostwriter. If I didn't find this career, I would have ended up with twenty different degrees and eighty different job titles because my curiosity is so great. I've always wanted to be everything, learn everything, and do everything. Okay, there are some things I have no desire to know more about, but most of the time, I'm fascinated.

Curiosity should be celebrated as a tool that can bring people together. Curiosity is what drives people to read memoirs. Curiosity is what allows us to walk up to someone in a coffee shop because they're wearing a sweatshirt with a message that interests us. Curiosity sparks conversations. Ultimately, it fuels connections.

Curiosity is wonderful, and I've had to remind my curious, little girl self multiple times that it's okay that she was curious. She doesn't have a dirty mind. She isn't dirty. She isn't shameful. She's just curious and that's okay. Any misguided curiosity can be redirected. There's more innocence and grace in that which I can now extend to her. Pure, childlike curiosity is one of the best traits we can have. I'm so grateful that it still stirs within me because it's one of my favorite parts about who I am.

quiet, not silenced

WE MOVED FROM MISSOURI TO A TOWN CALLED LINCOLN in Central Illinois for my dad's job. For about six months, all five of us lived in a single hotel room at the Comfort Inn & Suites. I would fall asleep on the floor as my dad watched episodes of *Married with Children*, trying not to think about the cockroaches. It wasn't that bad, but it's always unsettling to be in hotels, not knowing who—or what—walked the very floors we slept on. However, having an indoor pool made up for it a bit.

The move meant starting a new school in the middle of third grade. In the first week, during PE class, kids lined one side of the gym's divider line with giant, yellow rubber balls for the weekly dodgeball game. Since I was used to being the wallflower, I didn't expect to be a target. Dodgeballs flew at me, one after another, while mean kids taunted, "You talk funny." Illinois and Missouri may share a border, but Missouri is infinitely more "Southern." I stood out. Although to be fair, sometimes when I watch home videos, *I* can barely understand my accent.

I spent hours after school with Brittney, my new friend who became my best friend for the next several years, to break my Southern accent. The goal was to get me to attempt to talk "normal"—whatever that was supposed to mean. Now as an adult, I wish I didn't work so hard to shake it, because who doesn't love a good accent? Normal is boring, but it took me a long time to realize that.

For a brief period, I had a dream to become an actress. Since I loved losing myself in fiction stories as is, I wanted to embody the same characters that lived in my mind. When I finally worked up the nerve to try out for school theater productions, I was told my voice wouldn't carry across the auditorium. I tried competitive speech and enjoyed the oratory genre, but I couldn't nail the required nuance in inflection, tone, or volume to appease the judges. All I heard was, "You don't know how to talk right."

The only times I could elevate my voice was when singing. I spent hours upon hours pretending I was a singer, specifically as a fill-in for Mariah Carey and Paula Abdul. When by myself, I was convinced that I could sing *just* like them, as I headlined make-believe concerts, serenading whatever crush I had at the moment.

One evening, in fourth grade, I was invited to hang out with a group of girls. We were sitting on a trampoline, listening to music. Everyone started singing to Whitney Houston. I was hesitant to open my mouth at first, but then I joined in as we sang three songs in a row. I was so proud of myself for taking part and was having fun —until one of the girls singled me out. "Wow, you're, like, *really* trying to sing well, aren't you?" she laughed as she pointed at me. I wanted to be a good singer *so* badly that her words cut deep. I stopped singing around people after that. Even when singing happy birthday to people, I would only mouth the words.

It seemed everyone hated my voice. I did, too. So I continued to believe it was best to stay quiet. No one could make fun of me if they couldn't hear me.

I'm sure I was a quiet talker before the dodgeball incident, because my voice naturally doesn't carry, which is unhelpful when I have something to say. When it's noisy, my voice and entire body strain to reach a volume people can hear. I can't compete with noise, but noise is all around us.

When I'm raising my voice, my voice fills my head and clouds my thought pattern, making it difficult for my thoughts to come out as words. Then when I'm shouting to be heard, it apparently warrants the side eye and cringes as people look at me like I'm crazy. I don't know how it's possible to *only* ever be inaudible or too loud, but I don't know how to balance that in-between range. So I stay quiet.

I have an unfortunate history of staying quiet.

Quiet tends to be associated with weak and passive. So being naturally more quiet, and a woman at that, I allowed myself to play a weaker and more passive role than what my heart was actually calling me to live by. I've associated that narrative with my identity instead of realizing those are descriptors shaped by the world and not by truth.

I've learned that the process for reclaiming my voice starts by writing what I want to say. Then by reading it out loud. Then reading it again. I wholeheartedly believe that writing can help with processing our feelings, but there's a deeper release that comes with speaking it out loud. That's why I encourage clients to read their stories out loud after they've written them. It's a whole new level, and for many, a new type of deep healing that takes place.

Recently, I decided to invest in voice lessons. Originally the goal was to help me become a stronger and more powerful speaker, but it has evolved into so much more. The first few months were spent with my face beet red and me physically sweating, simply from doing the warm-ups because they were completely outside my comfort zone. They're such awkward exercises. She asks me to make weird noises and weird patterns with my voice stretching to both ends of my vocal range and beyond. The embarrassment of my voice had me wanting to run, but I was forcing my body to stay, and it was having a visceral reaction.

Over time, the awkwardness decreased. I became more comfortable with hearing my voice and learned to appreciate all the weird exercises for what they allow my voice to do. We actually moved our focus from speaking to singing, with playing the keyboard as well. I had to break through a very tall tower constructed with every self-limiting belief to sing in front of her, especially knowing I'm not a natural singer.

With each week, it became easier. I stopped sweating because I became less worried about how bad I sound and more focused on how each exercise will strengthen my voice. I sing in church now instead of just mouthing the words. I sing in front of people just because a song is on my mind. I don't hold myself to the expectations of being good because I still don't feel like I'm a good singer, but I sing because it brings me joy. I sing like I'm on that trampoline giving it my all, but not stopping no matter how many people are pointing and laughing.

What I've realized from the months of voice lessons is that my voice is more than just the tone or levels of which I'm speaking, but also the power of the words I use, and the authority in which I speak them. Trusting in the words I say, knowing that when I turn off my mind and speak or sing from my heart, it's all I have to do to get my voice to connect with my inner strength.

Even though I may naturally have a quieter voice, it's not a reason to stay silent or not to keep working on my voice. What started out as an initiative to become a better speaker has evolved into an understanding of the tone and pitch my voice actually has the capability to reach, leading me to discover a new "normal." My voice may never reach "loud" and that's not the goal. I've learned that my quiet voice can still speak with authority. I now speak when I have something to say and raise my voice, not in volume, but in strength.

Being soft-spoken is not a dilution of power; it's a refined force, capable of both introspection and profound impact. I no longer shy away from being quiet, but embrace it as a subtle power that can surprise people when they least expect it.

gifted, not inferior

SINCE THE TIME I WAS SIX YEARS OLD, I KNEW THAT BEING an author was my path.

I loved books. *Loved* books. I still do. A man will always win me over by buying me a book over a bouquet of flowers. A friend will win my heart by passing down a favorite book she knows I'll love, too. This past Thanksgiving, my mom gave everyone at the table a book. Some were funny, some were sweet, but the entire act had me in tears. I wish people would send each other books with hand-written notes in the margins or a summary of why that book helped them or changed them or inspired them. I believe sharing meaningful books is one of the most intimate exchanges we can have. To me, books are of equivalent importance to what money seems to be for most people.

One of my favorite traditions on Christmas Eve was picking out a gift to open that night. I would purposely seek out the present that felt like a book. I'd rip open the wrapping paper, anticipating which title would be in my hands. With the Christmas lights twinkling, I'd cozy up in a chair; it was my favorite place to read a book. Now, I crave the silence and peace of reading next to the lights the moment I put up the Christmas tree every year.

I'm not sure if my parents even knew at the time how those

books were fueling me. They gave my wild imagination someplace to play. They gave me new identities I could try out. They gave me friends when I felt I didn't have any. They gave me a portal to different time periods and countries. They gave me a dream.

One year, I received a big set of classic books with yellow spines ranging from *Moby Dick*, to *Wuthering Heights*, to *The Adventures of Huckleberry Finn*, among others. I sped through those babies, soaking up every word, amazed that something could be so *timeless*, stories that never get old no matter how the world changes.

I wanted to *write them*.

The first short story I wrote was called, *The Locker that Ate My Books*. It was *good*. It was creative and funny and above my level because I hadn't even graduated from cubbies to lockers yet. I even illustrated it on our computer, as I death-gripped the mouse and shakily outlined the boy, the locker, and the books with my embarrassingly poor illustration skills. Grit and determination pulled it off, and I was quite proud. We put it in a clear report folder with a burgundy plastic clip edge to hold it together. It was my first homemade book.

Somewhere along my many moves later in life, I lost the book. The last time I had it was when I lived with a boyfriend in Wausau, Wisconsin. I figure someday, it'll show up at an auction for a million dollars.

I didn't stop at one story. I kept writing. My imagination went crazy with ideas. My stories were something I could easily gift other people, like when I wrote my teacher, Mrs. Hannah, a story about her cat, Ozzy, based on the stories she shared in class. I'll never forget the tears in her eyes when I gave it to her and how she was so proud to read it to the whole class. She was one of my favorite teachers and the first person (besides my mom) who encouraged me to be an author.

Writing stories helped me work through my own emotions, like when I wrote *Problems in 6th Grade* when I was in sixth grade, disguising my truth as much as possible. It was about a boy named Milton who was being bullied, and the hero and heroine, Luke and

Rebecca, stepping in to help. Milton mirrored how I felt with my high-water jeans and getting picked on by a girl named Elizabeth who threatened to beat me up everyday. Rebecca mirrored who I wanted to be: a kind girl with beautiful red hair. Luke mirrored the type of guy I wanted to swoop in to save me.

My first Young Author Award was for a story about a girl who becomes best friends with a deaf girl. I was taking sign language classes at the YMCA with a friend, which became my inspiration. I won that contest three years in a row with a wide range of stories, and still have the blue ribbons. I also won first place repeatedly in the Science and Social Studies Fair during that same three-year period, for projects ranging from a paper mâche mummy as I showcased mummification to an interactive flashing lightning display, with actual thunder noises. (My mom spent hours with me as we took the thunder part of "The Thunder Rolls" by Garth Brooks, playing it on one cassette tape while recording the noise on another cassette tape, over and over, because that's how we had to do things back then.) Yes, I have those blue ribbons, too. Apparently, fourth through sixth grade is when I peaked in life.

In English class my junior year of high school, we were challenged to write a short story. I was stoked. I poured my heart into my first research-based fiction story about a boy who had the life-threatening Hutchinson-Gilford Progeria Syndrome and a girl who became his best friend. I had recently read an article about a boy who had it and I couldn't stop thinking about him. I created a character based on him and turned the plot into a story with an inevitable, sad ending. But it was powerful because of his many happy moments, since he didn't let a moment of life go by without being grateful for every minute he was alive.

The teacher asked for volunteers to read their book. My stomach turned in knots as I considered if I could stand in front of my peers and read my story. Slowly, I raised my hand to volunteer, half-hoping she would call on someone else. She called on me, though. I stood up, my knees shaking, and walked in front of the class. Clearing my throat, I tried to raise my voice so everyone could hear me as I read my story, word by word, line by line, page by page.

When I got to the last word, I flipped the stapled page over, my hands still shaking. I looked up at my class and saw tears. *Tears.* Even the boys! They all applauded and stood up after I was done. It was monumental! I was so proud of myself. I thought, *Yes, I'm an author. This is what I was meant to do.*

That high lasted two days. I received the paper back from the teacher, and it was marked up in red with a big C- written right next to the title of the story.

Keep in mind, I was a people-pleasing, A-student, goody two-shoes. I had just read a story that *moved* people—that made them *feel* things!

And it only warranted a C-.

I was humiliated. I remember looking at the teacher with tears in my eyes, my chin trembling. She looked back at me, a grown woman in her late 30s, wearing braces, with expressionless eyes. My eyes dropped to the braces poking between her lips because the embarrassment was too great. She didn't say a word.

I walked away believing I simply wasn't good enough to make it as an author.

I stopped writing stories for about eight years after that. My author dream faded because I believed I didn't have what it took after all.

I find it fascinating that I've known since I was six years old that I wanted to be an author. I knew God gave me that dream. Many people spend their whole life searching for their passion and purpose, but I was crystal clear on mine.

Yet I still managed to get off track with that dream. Why? An English teacher. Yes, someone you would think would fuel future authors, completely stamped out my fire.

Listen, some people will be told that they can't do something and will fight to become the best they can be. Others will roll over.

I rolled over. As though her opinion mattered above anyone else's simply because she held the red pen.

But we do that, don't we? We let one person ruin our dreams.

With my writing, I discovered that yes, grammar is not my strength, and no, I don't have any desire or interest in perfecting it. However, there are these amazing people called *editors* who *love* all those things and they're the ones scoring A+'s in English class. Editors help authors deliver an outstanding book that doesn't just have an amazing story, but has amazing grammar as well.

"I'm terrible at grammar," is something I hear from people who want to write a book as though it's enough of an excuse for why they shouldn't be an author, and I call it out each time. *I'm* terrible with grammar, but it's not a reason to ignore the calling on my heart. I get better with each hour I spend writing and with each book I complete, as I learn from my editors' corrections, but grammar will never be an area I feel like an expert in.

An author is not someone who can nail grammar; an author is someone who can craft a captivating story or message that connects with the audience they've set out to reach. Just like we need help publishing that story, we need help with the writing, too, and there's nothing wrong with that. It just proves how much stronger and better we are when we work together. It's one of the many things that fascinates me about how our individual journeys intersect, and how we all are born with such unique-to-us gifts. We're meant to work together; not alone, *especially* when it comes to the dreams in our hearts.

inspired, not regretful

SONGS HAVE ULTIMATELY BEEN THE BIGGEST INSPIRATION behind most of my book ideas. When I'm listening to a song, an entire scene unfolds in my mind, like my own version of a music video for it. One song has prompted the creation of an entire book, or in the case of *The Last Look*, it was all of the Jimmy Eat World "Bleed American" album which could be the soundtrack of that book. Most of the time, the vision developed because a song instigated a desire within me for a storyline that wasn't happening in my life, or one that played into my biggest fears.

Take the example of one of my favorite songs growing up, which was "God of Wine" by Third Eye Blind. Their self-titled album was my favorite for most of my life. Even to this day, hardly any album has hit me and shaken me up like that one did. From the first chord, I would stop everything around me and just sit, frozen, except with a few tears trickling down my face.

"God of Wine" struck me because I connected with the temptation to numb myself, to push away anything that mattered, because it all felt too big and too much. I found myself doing that with boys, with alcohol, with anything that could immediately create the feeling of my body disconnecting from my soul. It made me think, *What would this world be like if we all lived without emotions?*

That's how *The Remedy Files* was born, my young adult dystopian trilogy and first full-length book I wrote. The heroine, Evangeline, realizes she's born into a world without feelings, the very things that make us human.

When I read *The Giver* by Lois Lowry at nine years old, I was gripped by this idea of a false world, one devoid of the truth, yet the group in power knew the truth. On the surface, it was utopia, but severely lacked integrity and ethics, so the question was always, what's *actually* a better world?

The Giver rocked me and I read it at least once a year thereafter. So it's no surprise my first published novel was influenced by it.

With *The Giver* and "God of Wine" as inspiration, *The Remedy Files* was very much alive in my head. I was always thinking about the characters. They were regularly conversing in my mind like the imaginary friends they were. I had goosebumps for months as the scenes played out. I *was* writing it... but then I kept putting it off. And putting it off. And putting it off.

I chose to do other things than sit down to write. Meanwhile, the dream of this book was weighing on me, like a boulder growing bigger on my chest, suffocating me. Literally, every year, I felt like it was harder and harder to breathe deeply. All because of this dream that wasn't being fulfilled because of whatever excuse I had at the time, but it all boiled down to not taking action.

Many people say that writing a book is like birthing a baby and I think that's accurate.

The dreams, the love, the pain, the doubt of whether or not you can actually do it.

The difference is, babies still come out even when you don't think you're ready for it. The labor with my first child was less than two hours. The labor with my second child was literally forty-five minutes. They didn't even have time to give me an epidural, so I was forced to have a natural birth when that wasn't my original plan. (I know my pain tolerance level.)

"He's almost here! Just keep pushing!" the doctor and nurses chanted during my contractions.

"I can't! I can't! I can't!" I shouted back, wanting to give up completely.

In the worst moments of pain and discomfort, I didn't think I could do what it took to birth him.

But he came out anyway, because that's the way nature works. He had a destiny greater than the obstacles I faced to birth him. He's meant to be in this world, and there was nothing I could do to hold him back from that.

That's where birthing books is different from birthing babies. Books don't just come out because the time is right. We have to "labor" in pain until we push it all the way out. But many aspiring authors are yelling, "I can't! I can't! I can't!" And since our bodies aren't pushing our books out automatically, we're able to give up and walk away.

The one thing that isn't different is the fact that this world *needs* these books because these ideas were given to us for a reason. It becomes heartbreaking when we purposefully step off the path, waving a white flag, instead of staying committed to the mission.

The Remedy Files took an unnecessarily long twelve years to birth. It wasn't meant to take that long to be given life.

Inspired ideas land on us for a reason.

I had a massive wake-up call with *The Remedy Files*. After all those years of putting it off, I missed the reason why it was fighting so hard within me to be born: there was an international wave of dystopian interest coming. *The Hunger Games*, *Divergent*, and a slew of other stories made it big, going from published books to box-office hit movies.

And here I was, with an amazing book idea, but it was unfinished. I missed the boat.

I started *The Remedy Files* five years before *The Hunger Games* books were released. FIVE YEARS. What would have happened if I finished and published it before the dystopian craze arrived?

I spent a lot of years in regret, wondering that exact thing.

When I finally finished and published *Illusion,* the first book of the *The Remedy Files* series, the amount of reviews that compared it to some other dystopian book was disheartening. I was frustrated that I wasn't more disciplined and heartbroken that people would never see it for what it was. My series was considered a knock-off when it could have been—should have been— an original.

But I ignored the calling.

We all have unique gifts and they are different for a reason. Those gifts produce inspired ideas that only we can bring to life in our special way. We know when we feel the calling and when we ignore it... which is when we regret it.

That regret almost kept me from writing more at all, but instead, I knew it was more of a reason to dig in, and never have that feeling return. The only way to do that was by making sure I changed my ways. The one thing I've learned from all my mistakes is that if I miss one opportunity, it may feel like it's the end in the moment, but it's never too late to turn it around, to try again, to create a *new* opportunity.

Sometimes we get so focused on one door closing that we don't see the millions of other doors that are popping up around us. We just have to keep our eyes open. Regret can blindside us, but it doesn't have to *bind* us.

I could have given up on being an author after that happened, especially after some of those reviews I received. Instead, it motivates me to ensure that the next time a golden idea lands on me, I pay attention and get it done.

It's how my Golden Butterfly Theory was born. I believe we all have these little inspired ideas, called Golden Butterflies, that land on us. The butterflies choose us because of our individual perspective, path, feelings, voice, experiences, and gifts. It knows that it takes that unique combination for the idea to come to life in the most magical way.

That butterfly *chooses* us and brings us a specific purpose to carry out. Whether that's an idea to help others, give them hope, inspire them, guide them, persuade them, uplift them, open their eyes, or give them strength, the Golden Butterflies deliver these ideas to the right person at the right time.

When we don't bring forth the creation we were supposed to create, that butterfly will fly off us and land on another person. No matter what, the idea *must* come to fruition, because it is meant to help others, so the Golden Butterfly seeks out the right person who will be disciplined enough to bring the idea forth instead.

In all the hours and years I spent doing things other than writing, I was searching for something else to fulfill me when my dream was waiting to be fulfilled, and would have been exactly what I was searching for in those moments. We spend so much time searching for fulfillment externally, when we're sitting on a pile of gold within ourselves already. If more of us just gave those ideas delivered by the Golden Butterfly our all and didn't stop until the calling was completed, there would be real magic happening in our lives every single day.

When I started *The Remedy Files*, I knew the main concept, but it took a lot of writing to flesh out the meat of the story itself. It's one of the things that made me pause and restart over and over. The Golden Butterfly doesn't immediately bring clarity—it just brings the idea. It's up to us to then set out to do the work, even if that means wading through the muck to get there.

Many first-time writers get frustrated because they feel they're getting words down on paper, but their vision isn't as clear as they hoped. What these writers need to understand is that all of that writing is still inspired. These hours of writing are helping us uncover the core message, the core story, the core purpose of what we've set out to write. The process is helping us become better writers. We need to believe that since the butterfly chose us, we're already equipped with everything we need; we only have to trust our gifts, commit to the process, complete the calling, and watch the magic happen.

It's really that simple, if we only get out of our own way.

aware, not fearful

WHILE LIVING ON THAT DIRT ROAD IN MISSOURI, WE HAD stray cats *everywhere*. Underneath the propane tank in the backyard seemed to be the perfect location to burrow and birth their kittens. It didn't take long for the cats to multiply like gremlins when they're wet.

The first cat I grew an attachment to was Snowball, a beautiful white short-haired cat. He was my favorite for many years. Snowball eventually stopped showing up, and I was told he ran away.

For some (completely insane) reason, I was exposed to terrifying movies like the original *Candyman*. I'm sure it was due to having two older brothers. In fact, I didn't see it just once when I was a child—but *twice*. For those who have never seen it (and I beg that you do not), a woman is investigating the myth of Candyman, a man who appears and murders people when they say his name multiple times in a row while looking in a mirror. It's horrific as an adult to watch, but traumatizing as a child.

There is a scene where the woman walks into an apartment and it's a gory multiple-homicide. One of the victims is a beheaded dog.

Thanks to *Candyman*, for years after Snowball ran away, I would have nightmares about walking into a wooden outhouse out of all things. White fur everywhere. Blood everywhere. The head of a beloved cat.

Once in junior high, some friends and I were gathered to watch *Urban Legends*, because apparently being terrified was the cool thing to do. The moment a character put a dog in a microwave, one of the boys pulled the VHS out of the player, took it outside, and threw it in the bushes. Yeah, that's exactly how I felt. Thank God a man stood up for what was horrifically wrong instead of pretending it didn't affect him like every other "macho" guy was doing.

Now, when an animal shows up in a movie or a book, my anxiety takes over and I can't focus on anything except what may happen to the animal. Usually, I'll stop reading or watching it right away. To this day, I have a fear of what the kids may put in the microwave—and no, it won't be an animal because they're not soulless, but it opened my eyes to what *could* be put in there.

While we lived in the Comfort Inn during those first six months in Lincoln, I became fearful of the pool. I realized I couldn't see the bottom of the deep end, so naturally I assumed sharks were in there. Yes, *Jaws* had infiltrated its way into my mind. I wouldn't swim any longer because the fear took over reality.

As I've gotten older, despite now avoiding horror and high-violence films, my fears have gotten greater. These days, I not only fear sharks in the pool, but also alligators. Not to mention, new fears have multiplied as quickly as those stray cats.

I wouldn't be surprised if by the end of this memoir, I reference a hundred things that I have a fear of.

These fears have turned into a puppeteer for much of my life—they control my actions. It's as though I've turned control over to them, letting them guide me. But the truth is that fear will never get me to where I am called to go.

I had dreams when I was younger to graduate college and then travel to different countries, live with the people there, work like them, learn from them. I was going to fully immerse myself in those cultures and write about them. Then, save enough money to go to the next country and do the same. But fear stopped me. I worried about traveling alone. I questioned how I could be accepted in other communities when I barely felt accepted in mine. I feared offending people of cultures I wasn't yet familiar with. I feared being sexually assaulted. I didn't know how to be okay in any place other than my small, little world.

I wonder with all that we've seen in our lifetime, from war to constant mass shootings in every single place we once called safe, if all of us have a heightened awareness of our surroundings, as indirect and direct trauma. When the Columbine shooting happened, I was at home sick. While laying on the couch, watching the live footage, I saw things they later cut out in replays—kids dropping out of broken windows just to get out, bloody. It was burned in my mind.

Once I became a mom, I moved into a state of perpetual fear. There seems to always be something to worry about with kids. In order to avoid constant heart attacks and from becoming a helicopter mom, I try to remind myself that there are spiritual beings watching over them, too. I'm not the only one responsible for their well-being. It allows me to breathe a bit more.

Some of my fears are warranted, incited by real-life events. Like the way I become tense and fearful when certain men get too close because of the violations and assaults throughout the years. Or how at a movie theater, I fear someone will start shooting, so I plan for an escape.

My imagination has been helpful in my creative endeavors, but is often a detriment to my daily life. My fears are as wild as my best stories. Imagining the worst happening means rarely being at ease. My eyes constantly dart around, preparing to act, working out my next steps to move when the bad thing takes place. I feel more in flight mode than rest mode. Most of my fears are putting energy toward the worst-case scenario simply because it *could* happen, which steals moments of joy and enjoyment I could have instead.

When I realized how many fears take up my thoughts throughout each day, I wondered how I haven't gone completely crazy yet.

In part, it's because of my writing. My writing has saved me time and again.

Much of my fictional writing is rooted in fears I have. When writing, I have a safe, controlled zone to allow those fears to play out and go to the extremes in order to explore the what-ifs. The process lets *me* have control over *them*. They're not always extreme fears, but even more minor fears like fear of not being good enough, of not being accepted, of not being loved, of failing.

I also see my fears reflected in other people, which helps me identify previously unrecognized fears to take quicker action.

When I'm reading people's stories, especially their first draft, I tune into the anxiety that pulsates underneath their sentences. It definitely comes out before they share their draft—they over-explain and apologize, peppering me with unnecessary disclaimers. In their writing, I can see them hiding or skirting around issues, not going deep enough when the story is calling for it, or covering up their own voice with AI tools because they don't think their writing is good enough.

I see authors wade in fear as their first reviews come in. They just published a freaking book, doing something that many people don't accomplish, and yet they let their excitement succumb to poor reviews from people who have never done the feat themselves. The authors will get one hundred glowing reviews but then they'll get one review from someone who hit on their biggest fear, and they will crumble, because now their biggest fear has been validated by one person, and not the hundred other people who loved their book.

I warn authors about these things in advance. I try to mentally prepare them for what's coming in hopes of strengthening them, and helping them see that those things aren't what matters. But sometimes we simply must live it to learn it.

At times, I can be hyper-aware, as I'm looking for signs of anything that could go wrong, with my finger hovering over my flight-mode activation button. But I've learned to considerably tone down that awareness, and use it as a tool to manage the fear instead.

Awareness can be one of the best partners when encountering legitimate fears, and also a superpower in controlling fears that are unwarranted. The quicker I'm aware of barriers or obstacles or setbacks in what I'm called to do, the quicker I can overcome them and reframe the narrative of how they appear in my life.

Awareness has taught me to recognize fears not as overwhelming forces, but as signposts that point towards areas of my life needing attention, understanding, and sometimes, a change in perspective. Just as we are the thinker of our thoughts and not our thoughts themselves, we control our fears; they don't control us. These days, I'm much more mindful and ready to take action when those fears arise. I do whatever I need to do so that they don't overtake me, and I retain control of walking the path I'm meant to go down. One thing I know for sure is that I don't want to miss another calling on my life or any moment of joy, and relenting to fear out of all things will not be what stops me.

enough, not lacking

I WAS RAISED IN AN ERA WHERE THE INTERNET WAS IN ITS infancy. I was typing ninety words per minute in junior high, thanks to my mom's community college's typing program, so I think my mom probably thought that's what I was doing on the computer most of the time. Typing.

However, in the age of AOL and dial-up, I discovered chat rooms. Now, these were the original chatrooms where profiles didn't exist—just usernames and people we didn't actually know on the other side of the screen. It was all about the conversation. We either connected or we didn't.

There were a couple of boys, identical twin brothers, who grabbed my attention with flirtatious messages that instantly had me attracted to them. David and Danny were skinny, dark-haired, tattooed, and in a band. The typical hot and "cool" indie band boys. I was only fourteen and they were a few years older than me. They set a new standard for the type of boy I would be drawn to for many, many years.

They wanted all the girls to know what they looked like, so they didn't hesitate to share their pictures, but I didn't share mine right away.

When I looked in the mirror, all I could see was a dorky blonde girl in high-water jeans. I could banter with the best of them thanks to skillful sarcasm picked up from my dad. I came off as bold when the words flew from my fingertips, but when it came to speaking in person, I was shy. They didn't know this.

I couldn't tell which boy I liked more. Whoever was giving me the most attention at the time—which varied. One would show interest, the other would show interest; back and forth. Even when we were all in committed relationships decades later, there would be late-night chats and comments out of the blue. "You are gorgeous. You haven't changed." I ate it up because it was always easy to slip back into the patterns of our early years. I had an indescribable longing to be connected with them—probably because the relationship came into my life at one of my most vulnerable points. A relationship between three people spanning decades that goes soul-level deep, and hands down, the most interesting dynamic I've had in my entire life, although toxic at different points.

David and I eventually formed a special bond that edged out Danny a little, and he was the one I chased for years. But before that took place, first, I had to show him a picture of me.

Around this time, I got invited to go with a group of girls to get a professional group picture taken. I was shocked that I was asked to join. I wasn't exactly part of a friend group but hung out with enough of them individually that they invited me to be a part.

It was back in the day when Coca-Cola backgrounds were cool, so that was the theme of our mini photoshoot. We did a few different poses, including one where we're holding our hands as though they're guns that we just shot and we're blowing smoke off them. While everyone else had serious faces, I'm laughing because I felt so dumb trying to mimic them.

It was a bit of an awkward photoshoot anyway but while everyone else knew how to pose, I didn't. My body contorted within itself, my smile was half-forced, and my cheeks were red as I clearly felt uncomfortable. I remember thinking, *I'm going to ruin this picture. Why did they invite me?* I felt ugly. I didn't know what to do with my hands. (Yes, this is a recurring concern in my life.) I literally shrank from the camera.

Those were the only recent pictures I had. No way was I sharing it with David and Danny—or with anyone. I needed a different picture to show them, so I came up with a plan.

There was a girl in my grade who was the most popular girl. She was beautiful, sweet, an A+ student, played sports, was the Homecoming queen—basically the perfect female leading character in any book or movie. Everyone fawned over her.

I asked her if I could take pictures of her to practice my photography hobby—a hobby that didn't truly exist, mind you. She said yes because as though being perfect wasn't enough, she was also genuinely nice.

I went to her big house located in a fancy neighborhood and met her mom who was equally as beautiful. We went to her closet so she could pick out some outfits to wear. I learned she and her mom wore the same clothes and exchanged them all the time. I didn't know mothers and daughters could do that. It wasn't necessarily about the clothes, but that they connected over something they could share which was a foreign concept to me.

We went around to a few different spots in her yard as I "practiced my photography." She was stunning and so natural in everything she did. She knew how to angle her body the right way. She knew what to do with her hands. She was simply captivating. Her hair was perfect. Her face was perfect. Her body was perfect. Her smile was perfect.

Once we finished taking pictures, the guilt of what I was about to do started to kick in. I couldn't look her in her eyes as I packed up my things to leave.

Afterward, I had the film developed at Walgreens, picked out my favorite one of her (they were all good of course), scanned the picture, and sent it via email to David and Danny.

"This is me," I claimed.

"You're so beautiful!" they both said. "Wow!"

Of course I knew that would be their reaction. It would be any guy's reaction to her pictures.

Y'all, this was before catfishing was a thing. This was also after I had tried cutting out pictures in a magazine of "normal-looking" models and scanning them, to see if I could pull off using those. (That didn't work.) This was just pure lack of confidence and self-worth and a desperation to be someone beautiful and confident.

I kept up the act for a few months, while avoiding the girl at school as much as I could, but I felt like I was constantly walking under a black cloud. It may be no surprise that pretending to be like someone else feels like total shit. As each day passed, I started to lose sight of any good in who I was because I was so focused on what someone else had instead.

I knew I couldn't maintain the lie. My stomach was constantly in a knot.

The guilt eventually won out.

I couldn't bring myself to tell the girl what I did. I tried multiple times, but I couldn't force the words out of my mouth. I was horrified by my actions and scared of the consequences. I knew if she found out, word would get around to all of our classmates, and I couldn't face that. I was terrified that everyone would see me for what I was: a fraud and someone that couldn't be trusted.

But I wanted to meet David and Danny in person, and my deep desire to be accepted by them in real life was greater than my fears, so I had to confess.

I had Brittney take pictures of me, although I never told her why I wanted them. Even though she was my best friend through grade school and junior high, I couldn't tell her what I did and how I was trying to redeem it. I picked out my best outfits. I tried to do my hair nicely. (Which was a challenge in itself considering I had no clue how to do my hair. One of my friends, Heather, would always have to do my hair for me in the girl's bathroom at school.) We went to Kickapoo Park and she snapped picture after picture: me standing by trees, sitting on a rock, posing on a park bench, the list goes on.

Once we developed the film, none of the pictures seemed good enough to send to the twins. I kept comparing mine to the pictures of my classmate with her confident and alluring poses. I couldn't match them. I didn't know how to be confident in my own skin. The pictures didn't reflect the girl I was inside, but they were all I had. So, I relented. Completely terrified that I was going to face rejection, I scanned the pictures, wrote David and Danny a note about what I did, and sent the real me to them.

Guess what? The real me was enough. "You're still pretty," David told me.

I finally met the twins in person during a college visit when I was eighteen. Yes, nearly four years later. Choosing Northwestern College in Iowa as my college for my freshman year was by no accident. It was forty-five minutes from where they lived and I wanted to be by them.

By the time I met them, I was convinced I was in love with David. There would be times that I would travel eight hours to visit them in Nebraska to watch one of their shows or just hang out. David knew I drove all that way for him, yet we'd go visit some girl he had a crush on at the time. Yes, he would actually take me to go meet whatever girl was in the picture. I would constantly make myself available to him, but I was the fill-in when there wasn't another girl. I spent years playing his games, waiting for him, and him knowing he had me hooked. Danny would usually rescue me when he knew David was treating me like crap. He'd invite me to his room since they lived together and show me his drawings or play music for me. He would take me for a drive when David would have a girl in his room. I regularly wondered if I picked the wrong twin. I used to have a vision of Danny and I sitting in a brightly-lit living room, him playing the guitar as I sat on the floor, leaning against his legs, writing.

But I didn't have a great picker. It's like I wanted the pain because that's what I was accustomed to feeling. So the more a guy hurt me, the more likely I was to want *his* attention and to be with him. Cue the start of my unhealthy relationship patterns where my character is the backup, the side chick, the "fill-in" until the woman they really want arrives.

My sophomore year of college, I became very close with one of the admissions counselors. He was tall, stunningly handsome, had a perfect, bright smile, and was genuinely nice. He had a glow about him that I wasn't used to since I was into emo boys. He wore suits for work and his dress shoes cost more than my entire closet. But I liked him most when he would change into jeans and a t-shirt at the end of the night. We hung out nonstop and eventually, it was clear there was more of a romantic interest between us. We started making out when we were together.

I thought we were in a relationship until he flat out told me that I was not marriage material, so he was still dating other women to actually find his wife. *I'm not marriage material.* I remember freezing as the words sank into my bloodstream and became a part of me. I mean, it tracked. I was at a Christian university, intentionally seducing men, pushing the boundaries of what they were taught was a good Christian woman whenever I could, so yeah, it made sense. I was a fill-in until the proper wife showed up.

When I was dating my first husband, I could feel the woman he dated right before me was still very present in our dating relationship. I knew she hadn't completely gone away even when we married. Want to guess who he married right after we divorced? Her. My feeling of unworthiness was so deep that I actually felt bad about the fact that I "interrupted" their relationship. I spent years tempted to write her a note and apologize for delaying their inevitable marriage. To apologize for stealing the spot when it should have been her all along—because I should have been the fill-in, not the wife.

The "good enough for now but not forever" position wasn't limited to romantic relationships, friendships were included.

In math class my freshman year of high school, I sat behind one of the prettiest girls in our school. She had long, dark hair, purple eyes from colored contacts, and was half-Italian and hilarious. She was part of the popular group, but she and I instantly connected like soul sisters. We could be dorky and goofy but also have the most mind-blowing, deep conversations. We could share every secret, every thought, everything with each other and were fully accepted and loved. She became my best friend for twenty-two years.

But despite being her best friend, I was the one she called when she had no one else, not the one she would choose first when everyone was around.

Even now, as I'm almost forty, I find myself staring in from the outside of groups I long to be part of. I want the closeness they have, I want them to know me as much as they know each other, and I want to know them the same. I'll get invited to some events, but I'm not in the tight-knit group text. I have wondered what it is about me that doesn't attract people to me in the way I'm attracted to them. *What makes people think I'm not worthy of more?*

The difference these days? When I notice this feeling arising, it doesn't hurt me or drive me to be anyone else other than me. Now I understand that who I am, inside and out, is enough on its own.

I spent many years struggling to rediscover who I was and reclaim those lost pieces. One podcast changed it all. A mentor of mine sent me a sermon from Damon Thompson, a pastor in Alabama, about the concept of "confident rest." Suddenly, two important truths clicked into place:

I am loved wholly and completely by the One who made me.
I have been gifted with the exact tools I need to be enough to serve my role in this world.

That lifted immense pressure off my shoulders. I realized I could move through this world just being who God made me to be and doing what God calls me to do, and I don't have to try so hard to be what I think everyone else expects me to be. I can rest because I'm already accepted by the One who knows everything about me and about everything I've done. I can rest because I'm still enough in His eyes to be fully loved.

Then all these things that feel like they *should* matter in the moment, suddenly don't.

I wish I could go back and show my younger self I have always been enough just as I was created. Maybe I didn't look like the typical Homecoming queen or play sports like the girls I envied, but I was fantastically creative, imaginative, and really funny. Instead of being so focused on what I didn't have, I wish so badly I could remind that little girl about everything she *did* have.

Perhaps some people like me are meant to drift, rather than have one constant group of friends. Just like I once wanted to travel from country to country, maybe I'm meant to be a "floater" more than I'm meant to be a permanent fixture in someone's life or in one close-knit group. It doesn't mean I'm lacking anything, preventing people from loving me, but that I have a different role to play, and that's okay. As long as I'm being myself and showing up when I'm called to show up because anything less is a disservice to me and everyone around me.

Do I still crave companionship on the deepest levels? Yes, with friendships, family, and a future spouse someday who all *choose* me despite them being able to choose anyone else, too. We all want to be chosen and we all are born to not do this world alone. But whether I have those close relationships or don't have them, it doesn't change the fundamental truths. I'm still enough, and as long as I continue to show up and be the most authentic version of me, I'm *always* enough.

beautiful, not ugly

By fifteen years old, my legs had grown faster than my mom could keep up with in jeans length and my hips weren't far behind. My waist never thinned out vertically, but my hips grew horizontally, and my legs decided they wanted to be the longest of all. Which made trying to find pants at JCPenney on a budget quite difficult.

I was only 5'6" but my waist was short and my legs were extra long. In ninth grade, I was sitting in a hallway, waiting for the classroom to be unlocked, when one of my male classmates said, "You have really big hips." Some skin of mine was showing beneath my shirt, the stretch marks making it more obvious that my body couldn't keep up.

The first time I saw a Delia's catalog and discovered that they had long sizes for girls, I knew I was seen. *Long! Those exist?! I don't have to wear high-waters all the time!*

Throughout junior high and high school, all I could do was gaze at the beautiful athletic girls and wish that I could look like them. They seemed to be the ones who had it all: strong bodies, beautiful faces, and the attention of all the boys.

I would go home in the afternoons and sob, wondering why I couldn't be as beautiful as them. There was one night where the desire was strong and overpowering. I wanted to be beautiful more than I ever wanted anything else in my life. I was crying out to God, the distressed plea was a borderline scream, the anguish was deep. I was willing to exchange *anything* if He could just grant me that one wish. I can't remember what my end of the bargain was; more than likely, I didn't keep it.

All I knew is that I wanted to be anyone other than me.

Starting in seventh grade, my thoughts drifted to death more than life. I felt exhausted all the time. I tried to keep up with all the other kids and be like them. It was small things like begging my parents for the next Starter jacket to fit in during junior high (even though they were weird-looking). And feeling the noticeable distance between me and a close friend grow as she talked about shaving or not shaving our "bushes" and what guys preferred freshman year. None of it made sense because none of what they cared about seemed to actually matter, and I felt perpetually ill-equipped to be among my peers.

I couldn't stand to look in the mirror. I hated getting dressed in the mornings. I walked through the halls avoiding eye contact with people. I hated feeling so sad, and that hatred for my sadness just made me feel more sad and hateful. I regularly contemplated the best way to get myself out of this world because I was convinced no one would care if I was gone.

My parents forgot to pick me up from a YMCA basketball team practice one evening. Besides already knowing I didn't belong on the team because I was terrible at basketball, that one error drove home the story that I'm forgettable because I was constantly looking for proof. That's all it took to add fuel to the fire. Pills. Cutting. A gun. Dropping my hair dryer in the bathtub. Train tracks. I experimented with all the ways I could kill myself, testing each one, but never quite doing it. Thank God I was such a fearful person because the fear of not being able to do it all the way through, where I'd have to feel an abundance of physical pain as well, is what kept me from completing the act.

My heart constantly felt heavy. Even though it was self-imposed,

I couldn't turn the self-hate off. I tried to smile. I tried to be what other people wanted me to be, but it was static-filled noise playing in my ears driving a temporary insanity behind the mask.

Until I turned fifteen and suddenly, I tuned in to a brand-new station.

My friends and I were hanging out at Steak 'n Shake, since that's what we did in Lincoln, outside of cruising the strip (driving up and down the main street through town) and watching terrifying movies. The extremely handsome captain of the soccer team, two years older than me, 5'10" with a solid build, brown, wavy hair, and blue eyes, was hanging out with his friends. His name was Aaron, and somehow, I caught his eye. I was handed a folded note from one of his friends saying that Aaron liked me. Of course at first, I thought there was no way that was true. A part of me was convinced that he was playing me, but I also immediately had a crush on him because all it took back then was a boy being cute.

However, he ended up being so much more than just a cute boy.

To this day, anytime my stomach starts to do flips, it takes me back to when I sat on the bench outside of the movie theater in downtown Lincoln. My mom had dropped me off, and I was waiting for Aaron to show up for our first date. I had to poop so badly because I was that nervous. Oh, it was bad. My stomach was making all sorts of loud, unattractive noises.

Aaron showed up, and smelled so darn good. I would later find out it wasn't cologne; it was just him. I'd crave that scent for years afterward. Not long ago, I went out on a date with a man who carried the same scent and the nostalgia gripped my heart. I would have married that man for his scent alone. (Spoiler alert: We didn't make it past one date.)

Aaron and I sat in the movie theater, electricity sparking between us. Our arms rested on the same tiny arm rest, barely touching. I could tell he wanted to hold my hand, but he didn't. I couldn't focus on the movie. All I could feel was his heat.

Aaron had permission from my parents to drive me home after

the movie. We walked out together to his white Buick. The passenger door was jammed, curved in from an accident and wouldn't open, so I had to crawl through the driverside to get to my seat. The sheepish smile he gave me as I slid in the seat melted me.

It didn't take long before we were boyfriend and girlfriend, and I fell madly in love for the very first time.

Aaron made me feel beautiful every single day, and told me it as well.

He talked to me nonstop, sharing everything on his heart. He made promises that he kept. He would write me letters daily with each one saying "hay" instead of "hey." (Something I would let be a stupid reason to break up with him later.) He gave me my first kiss that actually meant something sweet.

He played the guitar and sang to me. He held my hand. He loved me. He took me to church and showed me what it was like to love God.

He was there when I was saved for the first time at the no-air conditioning, Black Baptist Church on a 100-degree day in Florida during a choir tour. He cried when they dunked me in the water and hugged me like I couldn't have made him more proud.

He serenaded me with a bunch of other boys in the rain outside our cottage during that tour.

He didn't care that I couldn't actually sing. He didn't care that I couldn't play sports.

He didn't even care that I wasn't all that nice to him very often. His super-tan, Arizona-living, wonder grandma threatened me if I ever left him and broke his heart.

So I did.

And I have spent years upon years regretting it.

I didn't love myself enough to love Aaron the way he deserved. I was so mean to him toward the end especially. I would sing "Little Black Backpack" in a needlessly threatening way. I ignored his calls. I accused him of cheating when there's no way he would have. I told him I was more in love with David than him. Yet he still refused to let me go. Eventually, I broke up with him for a bad boy named

Kevin who shouldn't have gotten an ounce of my attention. Kevin didn't take care of me the way that Aaron did, but Aaron's love and affection was too much for me. I knew I was doing something stupid, but I did it anyway. Aaron made me feel happy, and I wanted to go back to my place of pain.

Thirteen years after our devastating breakup, I had a brief second chance with Aaron. We reconnected through Facebook and then started texting and talking on the phone. His voice gave me the same butterflies I had when I was in my teens. He was moving from Arizona to North Carolina to pursue a new opportunity and was passing through Illinois right as I was going through my first divorce. The moment I saw him, my knees buckled and I couldn't catch my breath. He smelled the same. He even looked the same somehow.

I was in a not-yet-settled divorce and beyond lost. Not because of the divorce, but because I still didn't know who I was. I'm pretty sure Aaron sensed that because there seemed to be no romantic interest on his end when we hung out that night. The only thing racing through my head was, *How can I seduce him to keep him?* But he wasn't open to it. I questioned if he forgave me for being so mean to him and breaking his heart. His mom, who I loved like a second mom and stayed in touch with for a good decade afterward, had told me multiple times that our breakup wrecked him for several years. I hated that I hurt him when he had brought such a positive change within me.

What Aaron doesn't know is that I never got rid of the box of his letters. I still have it to this day, half-holding on to the possibility of some kind of crazy future love story.

One month after our second chance at romance, he called to tell me he met an Irish girl at his church and was sure he was going to marry her.

My first thought was, *God, please... don't take him from me,* followed by, *Okay, this is what I deserve.*

He was my first love and the cliché, but true, "one that got away."

Somehow, Aaron saw my beauty, not just externally, but internally, in a time I needed to be seen the most. He believed I was someone worthy of being loved. What I had craved so badly was in front of me and I threw it away.

It's crazy to think that I had a second chance with him thirteen years after our first chance, and I still wasn't in a position where I loved myself enough to love him like he deserved. It's sad to me that I had to hide behind sexual advances because I didn't trust that being myself was enough without trying to turn someone on. It makes me sad for the missed opportunity as much as it makes me sad for the girl who still couldn't get to the place she needed to be at after all those years.

Now... *now* I love myself. If I had a third chance with Aaron, it would be different. But he's married (yes to the Irish girl) with three kids, so that ship has sailed.

I still always think *what if*, though... It's hard not to. I'll look him up on Facebook every now and then. He still somehow looks the same, and I'm sure he still smells the same. I'm still able to hear his voice although it's been over a decade since I last heard him speak. I wonder why I didn't appreciate what I appreciate now... even down to the "hay" instead of "hey."

Aaron could have chosen any woman he wanted, but he chose me. It was the first and only time I felt that someone chose me and devoted themselves to me, even with knowing the good, bad, and ugly of what was inside. Aaron saw that I was beautiful in spirit and could see what I was made to be. He saw in me what I had yet to see in myself.

I'm forever grateful Aaron saw in me what I refused to accept. He taught me that real beauty is not just what's on the outside, but radiates from the inside. He showered me with light when I was swallowed by darkness.

Through the two years we were together, the transformation in me is documented in pictures. I went from being shy and cringy in pictures, to more bold. I stood straighter, smiled bigger, and didn't completely dread seeing pictures of me. I *liked* the pictures, especially when he was next to me. I stood confidently, knowing exactly what to do with my hands for once. I started to believe I could be beautiful.

All those years spent crying about how ugly I was, I now look back at pictures from that time and my lens has notably changed. In learning how to love myself, I've learned to love the little girl back then, too. I can see her heart. I can see her wishes. I can see her beauty.

capable, not addicted

I STRUGGLED WITH A PORN ADDICTION FOR ABOUT sixteen years of my life.

This is not something I would have admitted two years ago. Not many people in my life know about it. It's still hard to write about.

Because for women especially to admit that, it's a shock. It's definitely un-ladylike. But it was my reality while I tried to find who I was.

The first time I ever saw porn was when I was ten years old, Brittney and I found a raunchy magazine that belonged to her dad while snooping for Christmas presents in her parents' bedroom.

To this day, I remember the picture. Which is unfortunate— that out of all the memories that have escaped me, that's one that still comes to mind. I also hate that it has to be as clear as it is, but that's also a testament to the effect it had on me.

I immediately felt unsafe around her dad from then on. I didn't call it unsafe, but I called it uncomfortable. It's like I now knew what made him go to *that* place. Like a deep secret that we uncovered that remained at the forefront of my mind whenever he was around.

As uncomfortable as it was, it also instigated a curiosity. I wanted to see more, to learn more, to quench what was awakened within me. Oftentimes, I tried to find reasons to snoop again in their bedroom to see what else we could find. I think eventually her parents caught on because suddenly the magazines disappeared.

However, it didn't take long to realize I could also access similar pictures online. It was a far cry from when we first learned about this new thing called the internet while at school, and accessed innocent sites like Toys"R"Us that had games that could be played. I remember seeing that website for the first time, in awe of the way it slowly loaded on the screen with its bright colors and fun characters. With just a click of the mouse, we could access brand-new lands.

It's not like I searched for porn, but for the specific keywords of what I was interested in, starting with body parts or positions. I could easily clear the browser history on the only computer in the house so no one would find out. I did this night after night in junior high and high school, without my parents ever knowing.

Since I was driven by what I *thought* men wanted from me, I thought, *How cool would I be if I could be the woman who was into porn, into the same things that got them going?* That was not the compass I should have let lead me. Yet I did. I watched porn as though it was research and preparation to finally get the attention and love I was seeking.

Watching porn was something that I actually bragged about, as though it was a "selling point" for men to be with me. I used to try to get Aaron to watch it with me, and he wouldn't. He was the only guy who refused. Other men were all about it.

But soon, porn became something I couldn't stop looking at on my own. It stopped being just about the men I was trying to win over.

Sex filled my mind so much that I couldn't look at anyone without a sexual fantasy playing out in my head at the same time. Not of them, but a constant porn movie running in my mind, unable to shut it off. Sometimes I'd look at pictures during the day while working in busy offices. It also made me addicted to masturbation as a result, to the point that I once had a dildo delivered to an office that I was working at via instant Amazon Prime, and used it *at* the office. I couldn't even wait to get home. I didn't understand that compulsivity and recklessness like that aren't just careless and stupid, but a sign of addiction.

I didn't have any space in my head for anything but pornographic thoughts.

Simultaneously, it heightened my fear that every man only wanted me for my body and carried the threat to rape me. Again, it was the constant push and pull. I wanted to be sexually desired, but it all had to be on my terms. That push and pull made me crave more violent sexual relationships for a period, until I actually started fearing for my life after one brief relationship. That's when I realized the dangerous territory I was crossing into and that reality wasn't as fun as the fantasy.

A danger of the porn industry is how everything is fantasy-based. Even when portraying "reality," fantasy takes over and suddenly reality isn't good enough. It makes people constantly choose something temporary over reality. By doing so, it short-circuits what they're actually capable of being, having, and achieving. They're exchanging their own value with each view, with each second of participation.

What I didn't realize until now, with age and in hindsight, is how much that addiction devalued who I was made to be. I lessened myself by having to put other women and sexual actions at the forefront to win a man's approval. I never felt good enough to stand on my own and have that same effect on men, as though it was the only way to capture their attention.

Recently, while reentering the dating world, I became interested in a man who implied his porn addiction was in his *past*, something he broke free of. There was so much safety in the idea that this man did not have a porn addiction; that I didn't need to worry about it.

One day as we were texting, the exchange became sexually heated. I was insanely attracted to him *and* felt safe. It was something I had been wanting so badly to find, and thought I finally found it.

Until he used the phrase "dirty slut" in that exchange. It was like being on the Drop Tower at an amusement park. We were rising, rising, rising—and then it dropped and I wanted to vomit. In a matter of seconds, my haven turned into a battle zone, and I immediately picked up my shield. I knew that phrase. I knew it well. I knew he hadn't actually overcome porn despite all his big talk. That was the dead giveaway. I stopped responding and a couple of hours later, we got on the phone because he could tell he said something wrong. After asking him about it, he confessed that he was still giving into moments of weakness, including the moment we were texting.

I knew then that we wouldn't work.

My distaste for pornography has become so strong, that I am literally repelled by the idea of a man losing himself in it, in actually getting pleasure of any sort from porn. It stems from the part of me that I haven't yet forgiven as I very much hate that portion of myself.

This same man is an advocate for freeing women and children from the sex trafficking industry, yet he still indulges in porn, as do many people who play both sides of the coin. I didn't realize when I was addicted that it's all the same industry, but I know better now. You can't advocate for one side, saying how bad it is and how women and children need to be freed from it yet turn to the same industry when you need temporary pleasure. That's the part that has me the most sad about my addiction now. Not only the devaluing of myself, but also the promotion, indulgence, and contribution to an industry where not all participants have a choice, but it's all they've known, even for some, from the time they were a child.

Once you recognize that, you can't unsee it.

Someone asked me how I got over my porn addiction after so many years. It was something I had to fight for, and at times, I still have to fight against it, not even allowing myself to watch some movies because I know it will be a trigger. The simplest "trick" that worked for me was that I had to allow myself to become so completely repulsed by it that it caused a greater adverse reaction than the dopamine hit. And I did that by simply associating it with the same industry that generates child pornography.

Pornography doesn't discriminate between what's ethically right or wrong and it sets out to purposely convert every single person into someone that watches it no matter how morally wrong the subject is. As a mother, the loss of children's innocence creates a visceral reaction because I want absolutely no part in it. Especially after seeing the way perfectly good people were brought into the trenches of pornography. It's like literally watching people burn as they become ashes of who they once were, slipping into a private world with most not even telling their spouse that they're doing it.

We're in a society where it's a well-known fact that men struggle with porn. I'm in a place where I recognize that there's no way I can be in a relationship that includes a man who indulges in it—add that to all the other rare traits I'm searching for. I can't have someone who might bring me back into that world. I also want to find someone who recognizes what I see now: I only want God's best and I'm deserving of that. Choosing porn is *not* saying I want God's best. Not for me, not for the people starring in it, and not for my future significant other.

I have come to realize that I have a very addictive personality. I have to be careful. Whether eating sweets, drinking alcohol, gambling, binging TV, working, or seeking the attention of a man who I shouldn't be seeking attention from... once I get my mind on something, once I start indulging, it's hard for me to stop.

When we're stuck in an addiction, it does more harm than good because we lose our sense of balance. Addiction wraps around our throat like a boa constrictor. It's constantly threatening to cut our lifeline until we give in. It blocks out everything else, acting as though it's the one thing that will make us feel better. An addiction is also usually the one thing that will cause us to lose ourselves and everything else important to us.

When I felt I finally overcame the addiction—as in completely cut myself off and could turn away from it—I felt *free*. Holy cow, so very free. The continually running porn movie in my mind shut off.

The constant dirty word associations stopped. The dark fog in my mind finally moved out. Men became less of a threat and I actually found a few I could trust. I no longer touched myself inappropriately in the worst places to do so. I wasn't weighed down by constant shame that I was a woman with a porn addiction. It was like clearing out a burned down forest, allowing new trees to seed and grow.

I felt chained to this addiction for too long. In overcoming it, it's made me more aware of how easy it is to slip into an addiction when I don't value or love myself enough to realize I deserve more than what that addiction is going to bring.

If the temptation arises in the darkest of moments, I will myself to remember this feeling: the choice to say no. The choice to keep my worth intact by not succumbing to something that wants to strip it away. The choice that comes from the strength I have in protecting my mind, body, and spirit. The power that comes with choice, not with addiction.

imaginative, not delusional

My imagination has always been wild. Whether throwing bits of reality with it in a blender and mixing it up to get something unique or compounding the effect of already imaginative things to make them borderline crazy, my brain does not stop. It is constantly working to project a billion different variations of whatever is in front of me at the time. Pair that with being great at creating out-of-the-box solutions and the result is ideas for books bursting into my mind like popcorn kernels in hot oil. I am good at making things up, and books give me a place to apply those ideas in a slightly less crazy way.

I literally could just get paid to generate new book ideas for people. My clients tell me constantly that they're amazed by how my brain works. I listen to *how* someone speaks while they share their stories, their passion, their hearts, their minds, and I get vision after vision of books that can be created based on both what they're saying and not quite saying yet. I FREAKING LOVE IT. I'm normally a very mild-energy person, but you get me in book-creation mode and I become a giddy little girl.

My own stories fueled by my imagination run rampant as well.

Sometimes I wonder if I'm in a "Truman Show" situation, like a social experiment where the world around me is fake. The people in my life are paid participants and everyone knows the truth, except for me. I'm the experimental unit. Cameras are hidden everywhere and I'm just being watched, tested, analyzed.

Sometimes I wonder if I'm truly delusional and going through my life, living it, but what I *think* I see in front of me are actually delusions of my mind. There's a different world that I'm wading through and it's because some sort of trauma keeps me stuck in this memory of a life long ago, while whoever is around me, watching me, is saying, "She's living out this scene again. I feel so bad that her mind keeps her locked there."

Sometimes I wonder if my thoughts are actually all being said out loud and I don't realize it. I especially wonder this in group settings like church or conferences while a single speaker is on stage. *Am I saying all my thoughts out loud? Do people know just to ignore me because that's who I am, the crazy person who is muttering her mind while everyone else is silent?*

I've always had a mind that operates like this, but it's funny the way I've channeled those ideas throughout time. My imagination creates scenarios inspired by whatever it is I'm longing for at the time. If people really paid attention to my ideas, they'd notice a direct line to a notable void.

Love has always been one of the greatest instigators of my imagination because I wanted it, but I didn't have it in the way I needed it.

My dad and I had a strange relationship. I heard the story over and over about how he simply didn't know what to do with a girl when I was born. Imagine hearing that above all else: your dad didn't know what to do with you because you were a girl. It became yet another reason I didn't want to be a girl.

My mom's parents were divorced and both remarried. Her mom (my grandma) married a wonderful man named Dorsey, except I knew him as Grandpa Hoffman. They lived in Nevada, so I rarely got to spend time with them. This was before FaceTime or video calls bridged distances, so we simply didn't have a way to be present with them. But the few times I did get to see Grandpa, he would affectionately call me Smurfette and give me the best hugs.

When I was twelve, I flew out to Nevada to spend time with them by myself. That's when my period decided to start and I was completely unprepared on how to handle such a thing. My grandpa went out to the store to buy me pads and tampons without hesitation. He was a *real* man. He even had to call Grandma while standing in the aisle trying to figure out what to buy to ask if I needed small, medium, large, or extra large. I mean, I was twelve years old, so the size should have been apparent. But his valiant act always stood out to me.

My grandma later told me that I had upset my grandpa the day that I got off the airplane during my visit. When they watched me get off the plane with an older boy I had spent the whole flight talking to, my grandpa was pissed. I told them he was a nice boy and I liked him, but all my grandpa heard was that I was talking to a serial killer. He served as a Highway Patrolman so he'd been exposed to some really horrible things. The thing that stood out to me? My grandpa was protective of me. He loved me. He openly wanted the best for me. I really think that if we had lived by him, the way my life played out with men would have been different. I would have felt the love I needed instead of seeking it elsewhere.

Instead, I found it wherever I could get attention from men, in any way I could.

Despite my actions and missteps, I didn't acknowledge the void in my heart to feel loved by men. That is, until I met a woman named Brittany while I was working a corporate job when I was thirty. We went to the gym together after work one day, and she was talking about some boys who were pursuing her, and how she just knew they weren't good enough for her so she was turning them down.

I hit the stop button on the treadmill and gaped at her, eyes wide. *You can say no to guys?* I didn't realize I could actually be picky. It never quite occurred to me that I didn't have to accept whatever scraps I could.

Like in eleventh grade when I had a big crush on one of my friend's brothers, Mikey, who had an awesome laugh, bright eyes, and was in an emo band. No surprise there that I was attracted to him. We were all hanging out one night, including Mikey's friend whose name I don't even remember. Mikey wasn't interested in me; his friend was. I fell asleep at their house that night crushed that Mikey barely even looked my way. So when his friend pulled down my pants in the middle of the night and started performing oral sex on me, I didn't say a thing. I didn't want it from him, but I didn't say no.

When I was in seventh grade, I met a boy online from Indiana, and while my parents were at work, he came over. He did things to me that I didn't want him to do, but I thought I deserved it for inviting him over in the first place, especially after he drove all that way to see me. I had nightmares about him for a year after, and still to this day can't stand the name Brett.

In my late twenties, I went to visit a guy friend I had met during a work conference in Atlanta and he tried making a move on me. I told him I wasn't interested and he said, "But I've been driving you around all weekend, I deserve this." I let him do what he wanted and cried the whole time.

I had a lot of desires but no boundaries. Combine that with a lack of self-love and self-worth, and that's how these things take over without lessons being learned.

When I questioned Brittany what made her so strong, so sure of herself, she said, "I've been shown love by my dad and my brothers my entire life. I don't need it in a man when I already have it from home." She called her dad and her two brothers her best friends. They told her they loved her all the time. They called her all the time just to check in. They showed up to everything she did and told her they were her biggest fans.

Like a light bulb turning on, I realized that's why I had been so obsessed with the wrong boys for as long as I could remember: I was desperate for a man's love because I didn't feel the same stability of it in my life.

Instead, in junior high, I entered into fake relationships with boys in chat rooms. In high school, I was on the newspaper staff, and created a new section called Song Dedications. Students dropped dedications in my locker anonymously using only their initials. I'd regularly make up dedications to me from others, but no one actually ever dedicated a song to me.

My freshman year in college, I created personalized CDs for three men who I had crushes on, and sent them anonymously with an email address they could reply to if they wanted to know my identity. That inbox stayed empty. I always did things I wanted other people to do for me, then fell into a depression that would last for days at a time when the response wasn't what I'd imagined. Somehow, I always had hope they'd respond the way I would have if it was done for me.

Attending a Christian university meant strict restrictions on interactions between men and women, especially when it came to the dorms. I created an unofficial program for boys and girls to get to know each other better for one sole reason: to get closer to a man. There was a student who was a downright movie star walking among us and I wanted a chance with him. Strong arms, wavy brown hair, and a killer smile—it was completely obvious he was a California man in a small Iowa town. I tracked down a yearbook and learned his name was Craig. From the moment I saw him, my whole body tingled, so I knew I had to have him. He was a senior and I was a freshman so the chance of us ever ending up in the same room was slim.

The whole point of creating this program was simply to get his attention. I didn't care about anyone else. It was just for me to be set up with Craig for a few hours. By some miracle, he agreed to participate, so I was his partner by "luck of the draw"—meaning I completely manipulated it, of course.

Craig and I spent a few hours doing the planned scavenger hunt. He was as wonderful as he looked. He was very into nature so he asked if I wanted to go for a walk at a spot just outside of town a few days later. We took his beat-up blue truck with the crankshaft windows that took the power of an ox to roll down. I now knew why his arms were so strong. A man like Craig made a truck like that look downright sexy.

We hiked a few trails and chatted nonstop. Once we got to an open field, we sat down on the grass. Soon, a few deer came out to join us, wandering around mere feet from us, not caring that we were as close as we were. After the deer eventually walked off, we laid down on the grass and watched the clouds float by. A spider, the creation I'm most terrified of, danced across my stomach—*and I didn't even flinch!* There's no way I would let a spider crawl over my body in any other situation. But I was so at peace with Craig next to me that nothing else mattered. It was one of the most serene and beautiful moments of my life.

Soon, it started sprinkling (because this whole moment was purposefully designed to be like a dream). We laid there laughing, getting wet for a little bit, until we ran back to his truck to head back to campus.

I didn't believe in fairy tales, until I had that date with Craig.

We kept talking for a few weeks, meeting regularly for coffee, but I didn't know how to have a healthy relationship. All I knew was that I wanted him so the only way to win a man was by... yes, seducing him. Giving him my body. Otherwise he would run, right?

So he came to visit my dorm room, and I quietly locked the door when visiting hours ended so they wouldn't know he was still in there. I led him to the bed, got him under the covers, and completely took over what I could with him... I didn't want him to leave. We made out. Hard. Getting a bit too close to having sex. All while the movie *Spirit* (yes, the animated children's movie about a freaking horse) was playing in the background.

Drenched in sweat, Craig pulled away and said he had to stop. I could see it right there in his eyes—the disappointment, the fear of how dangerously close we got. He knew I pushed it too far. I knew I pushed it too far. He wasn't like the boys I was used to. He was more like Aaron.

Instantly, I wanted so badly to take back that moment. But I couldn't. I couldn't erase what I had now exposed him to. He knew what I was like. He saw my true colors.

Two days later, he told me our values were different so we shouldn't see each other. I could actually hear my heart shatter. Regret and shame washed over me. I wanted to be the woman he needed, and not the mess that I was. I didn't know how to stop being that version of me, and he didn't even know the worst of it. Not to mention the fact that I completely manipulated our meeting in the first place.

Craig was a unicorn, but there were many other men I've laid eyes on throughout the years and thought, *this one feels the way I do* or *he must be the one.* As I've gotten older and started processing my patterns, I had a moment of being scared that I've been completely delusional. I'm so quick to create entire stories from one scenario, and have manipulated situations so that it fits whatever narrative I created. I started questioning, *What is true and what isn't?*

What I realized is that I was forcing things to unfold. I seized what control I could. I did that in marriage, in relationships, in friendships, with job opportunities, and clients. The thing is, with all those things I forced, I was pushing out what was really right for me. I didn't leave room for the things God wanted for me. I kept trying to fill my basket with what I thought I wanted instead of seeing what God had planned to give me. Like with Craig, perhaps I could have one day been right for him, but I pushed it during a time when I definitely wasn't, and caused a door to irrevocably close.

Historically, I operated from lack. The lack of love being shown from the men in my life. The lack of friends. The lack of acceptance. The lack of money. The lack of understanding. There was always a very specific lack that caused my imagination to create situations that just weren't true—but I wanted them to be, so I did whatever I could to make them be.

Manifestation has been a trendy word over the past decade, and I'm so grateful that despite all the things I imagined, they didn't actually come true, despite how badly I wanted them at the time.

Now instead of letting my imagination go wild and forcing

these stories into reality, I am more intentional in asking what God wants for me. I'm so tired of anything less. So, it means listening to His voice, keeping my eyes open to the opportunities, places, and experiences He places in front of me, instead of pushing something premature to take its place.

My imagination is one of my superpowers when used in the right ways. I've learned that instead of believing every single narrative my mind conjures, I take the time to recognize the source, and if it's from a place of lack or a place of God. Then, if I need to, I spin it into a fictional story instead of forcing it into reality, which is a much healthier outlet. I can get as delusional as I want when writing fiction and I love the freedom of being imaginative in any way I can without consequence, embarrassment, or shame.

Writing is the absolute best tool for an overactive imagination like mine. If I can go through life with pen and paper in hand, I maintain a much healthier state of mind.

loyal, not evasive

When I was twelve years old, we were visiting my dad at the trailer he lived at while he worked in southeast Iowa. When we opened the door, there was a tiny tabby kitten waiting for me on the table. Despite growing up with stray cats everywhere, my dad was not a cat guy. So seeing a kitten *in* his trailer was a shock. It was also an extremely sweet gift coming from my dad since I knew it was very much unlike him.

I still remember falling asleep with the kitten on me that night, its little claws nipping at my skin through the blanket. I named him Peanut Jr., since my family would call me "Peanut" as a little girl. Apparently Peanut Jr. was as creative as I could get. Somewhere deep inside, I must have known that he'd be the one pet that would become an extension of me because of what he became for me.

Peanut and I had a super close bond. I loved that cat with my whole being. He was special. Perhaps he was my first belief in the concept of "meant to be," because that cat was mine and I was his.

Peanut used to drag my underwear out from my unclean clothes basket and carry it all the way downstairs anytime I'd leave the house. He'd knead at it with his little paws. That was embarrassing. All sixteen years of his life, I'd have to worry about finding pairs of my worn underwear throughout either my parents' house or any other place I lived. Imagine walking in with guests and having to be prepared to kick a pair of underwear somewhere that couldn't be seen.

Peanut was my one constant through some of the most significant moments of my life. He was with me when I became a teenager. With me as I went to college. With me when I moved states and towns multiple times. With me as relationships started and ended. With me in the moments depression had me buried under the blankets for days. With me when I wasn't sure what else I actually had.

Peanut would crawl on my chest and snuggle, although he really liked sitting on my shoulder the most.

I loved that cat so darn much. Tears well in my eyes even now, thinking about him.

Toward the end of his life, he peed in random places and rapidly lost weight. He had a severe bladder infection and the vet recommended putting him down because even medication wouldn't lengthen Peanut's life long enough to matter.

Having to make that decision to end his life wrecked me. I can still see him drifting off to "sleep" as I pet him. For years afterward, I'd cry anytime I said his name. There were many nights I would still feel him in my bed. Truly, the blankets would shift as though he was kneading the blankets and I'd know it was him. I never found any of my underwear lying around though, otherwise I'd be sure he was still in spirit form.

I've never had as strong of a connection with an animal as I did with Peanut. It may have been why I was never able to hold on to any animal after him, why I sadly relinquished more dogs and cats than I care to admit.

Maybe that "one-time connection" is why I have yet to find someone who I can spend my life with after finding Aaron at fifteen, and losing the chance with him again when I was twenty-eight.

Maybe that's why I haven't had a best friend since the one who left me after twenty-two years.

Maybe when it seems that I can't commit to a relationship, perhaps it's just because I've loved hard once before—be it man, best friend, or pet—and I doubt if I can give myself over so fully and love like that again. The pain from those cut so deep, and I was terrified to love to that extent where it felt like there were parts of my heart that I will never get back, no matter the years that pass. I'm loyal to the "firsts" but I operated from a place of fear-avoidance with anyone who came after. I kept it safe, refraining from the passionate and deep love that I crave.

My grandma surprised me recently by asking, "Do you even want to be in a relationship?"

At first, I was shocked that she would ask that... and a little hurt. But I also know the way my life appears. I know what my choices imply. I knew exactly what she meant.

Do I truly want what I say I want when it comes to love or am I someone who will always do life alone?

I've had to get real with myself on my expectations in relationships that I enter and be honest about whether I'm planning an escape route from day one. That's a dangerous operating mode to be in, but it's one I assume out of self-protection.

Leave first before they get tired of you.
Leave first before you can see that you were never special or important to them.
Leave first before they leave you.

I've had to get clear about whether I'm projecting what I *think* they're feeling onto them, instead of really knowing and asking how they feel, and believing them when they tell me.

I've had to take stock of the people who are in my life and realize that just because they hurt me once in the past, it doesn't mean they'll hurt me again in the same way, so to stop expecting that they will in every encounter thereafter.

I've had to assess whether I'm assuming someone who has no

relation to someone who has hurt me in the past will hurt me in the same way just because they're in the same role.

I've had to realize that I can't have a present fear of not being given the same love, respect, and loyalty because of the stories or patterns of my past. Every day is a chance for a brand new story.

I've had to discover that not all love will be the same and that it *should* always be beautifully unique.

I've had to learn that death is a real part of life and accepting it means giving our love even more to those that we love, not less. I can no longer be worried about how much it's going to hurt when they eventually pass.

I've had to decide about what I really want in this life and what I'm willing to give. Because the truth is, I don't want to live life alone and I don't want fear to overrun love.

I've had to reset my loyalty to include more of what we're *supposed* to experience in life: heartbreak as much as the love, sadness as much as the joy, and being committed to experiencing it all in order to be alive.

I can't avoid being hurt, but I can make more intentional choices. Otherwise, the alternative is rejecting and withholding love in every form and that makes for a sad life to live. I've been there and don't plan to go back.

As I've worked on loving myself more, I've expanded my capacity to love others (because that capacity is a gift in itself) and to feel unshaken even if that love is not returned the way I may have hoped. When I go as far as to remove every single barrier, every single fear, every single expectation, every single worry, and fully surrender to the love I feel for someone, I stay loyal. I don't consider whether or not I'll be hurt by them in the future. I just enjoy that they're in my life.

I want to exude love because I finally feel it overflowing within me as well and don't want to hold back or limit the number of people (or animals) I can love. I'm not as reliant on what other people can fill me with and more trusting of what I can give regardless, and that has enriched my life and soul to no end.

guided, not impulsive

W HEN I BOUGHT CDs, I COULDN'T WAIT TO OPEN THE inside jacket and read the lyrics. The music was great, but the lyrics stopped my heart. I didn't want to miss a single word. Sometimes, I would make up my own lyrics, convinced I could have written a better song if they used my words instead.

When I temporarily stopped writing stories after the "you suck at grammar so you shouldn't be an author" English class fiasco, I leaned heavily into songwriting instead. I didn't know how to play an instrument, but always wanted to. Instead, I let my talented musician friends handle that while I focused on lyrics. I still refused to sing in front of people, but I could hum enough of the music that would randomly show up in my head that, when paired with the lyrics, they were able to reproduce it on guitars and sing it for me.

I was very much into indie and alternative bands for most of high school and college. Anytime nostalgia kicks in, I'll turn to my old favorites: Third Eye Blind, The Get Up Kids, Matchbox Twenty, Jimmy Eat World, Taking Back Sunday, Dashboard Confessional, Saves the Day, Eve 6, Jack's Mannequin, New Found Glory, you get the idea. Listening to those bands still manage to make my world stop and I have to remind myself to breathe. Meeting

Brandtson during my college years at one of their shows was one of the highlights of my twenties. I sent them lyrics to a song called "Bare Naked" that I was working on after meeting them.

"This is really good," they told me. "You should keep going." That was the only stamp of approval I needed.

I transferred from Northwestern College in Iowa to Olivet Nazarene University in Bourbonnais, Illinois for my sophomore year. I worked at a music store which was the perfect job for me. I studied my ass off to learn everything I could about every genre, every artist, every album, every song. Customers could walk in and ask, "Which album is this song on?" or, "I heard this song on the radio the other day, and these were the lyrics but I'm not sure who sings it," and I'd direct them to the exact CD.

I mean, it was a music store, but I wanted to excel because music hit a piece of my soul that made my toes curl. Since I wasn't going to be an author anymore, apparently, I started to consider becoming an artist and repertoire representative, planning a move out to Seattle to make it happen. I also had a knack for movie soundtracks. I'd watch a movie and think, *No! This song is all wrong for this scene. They should have picked this song instead.* I mean, that would have been the *perfect* job for me at that point in my life.

By my junior year, I was accepted into a selective music program hosted on Martha's Vineyard. I was chosen for my songwriting; other people were selected for musical talents including singing and production, and the goal was to record an album together by the end of the summer.

The summer before my junior year, I had moved in with some man that I met online. His name was Brian and he was eight years older than me. He was this seemingly-brilliant life coach, before life coaches were what they are today. The company he ran with some guy named Lou was ahead of their time.

Brian guided me to take an assessment that helped people discover what they should do with their lives. My results pointed me into the direction of counseling. I could see myself being good at that. People always wanted to talk to me about their lives as was.

After doing some research, I landed on becoming a marriage & family therapist with plans to go to graduate school to pursue a counseling degree.

Brian lived in this awesome factory-turned-loft in Villa Park, so Peanut and I moved in with him. Deep down, I knew something was off with Brian. Things always felt a bit uneasy despite his outwardly successful appearance. I mean, he wore suits and dress shoes every day even when working from home—he was a "real man!" I was in la-la-land, just going through the motions of what felt like "adulting." Besides, by now it's obvious I felt most comfortable in the places where I knew something bad was just around the corner.

I managed to get a job as a delivery truck dispatcher about ten minutes from the loft. So I'd go to class, go to work, and then come back home to Brian, who was usually always working at his desk in the middle of the loft.

Despite the sexual ventures from my younger years, Brian was the first person I chose to give myself to. He's who I consider my "first." I wasn't exactly in love with him, but it felt like it was time. I was about to turn twenty-one, so it was a year of major milestones. Might as well add consensual sex to having my first legal drink. *The man was letting me live with him and bring in a cat and litter box to boot! I should finally do it.*

So we did... awkwardly... and while I was on top, he fell asleep.

My first time having sex, after spending years traumatized by the act itself, I willingly chose to give myself to someone... and he fell asleep. All I could think was that next time I had to bring in porn, because clearly I wasn't enough by myself.

With Brian and I becoming more official because there was some sort of false loyalty in my head now that I gave myself to him, and me now pursuing a new career path as a counselor, I turned down the summer songwriting opportunity the week before I was set to leave. I grappled with it for days, ultimately using Brian as an excuse. I didn't want to leave him. Although I think truly, I was scared of failing. I was going to be the person writing the songs for everyone else. *What if I couldn't live up to the high expectations?*

Fast forward a couple of months later when I discovered that Brian's ex-girlfriend, who he was still very much in love with, lived in the same loft building. We ran into her while taking a walk together on the trail that ran in the back of the loft, and he immediately dropped my hand. The clue that something was still going on with them should have been when we went over to Brian's mom's house. She pointed out the picture of his ex-girlfriend on her wall of photographs and mentioned that she still spoke to the ex every day. Apparently, Brian had been talking to her every day, too.

I passed on an incredible songwriting opportunity to stay with a man who fell asleep the first time we had sex.

My first time having sex was with a man who was cheating on me.

I'm not sure which way of wording that is worse.

And yet I stayed, because why not? There were nights we'd get in such bad fights that I would sleep outside in my Jeep. Yet that was more comfortable for me than declaring my worth and walking away.

I eventually got smart and broke up with Brian, moving Peanut and myself to scary, run-down, crime-filled Kankakee. I moved into a small room on the second floor of a run-down house that was converted into an apartment, just trying to make it by while I finished out school. It was a stark contrast to the luxury I had just been living in. There wasn't much in it because I didn't have much to my name. But I did have a keyboard. At that time, random songs would still pop into my head, so I tried to play them without actually having the musical talent to do so. It wasn't long after that the music stopped though. I sold the keyboard and got rid of what else I could to move on to the next location. It was in that transition that I let go of songwriting and started focusing on writing books again. *The Remedy Files* was alive in my mind.

After I graduated from college, I moved to Grand Rapids, Michigan since I knew a few people who lived in that area. I got my first job working at a printer supplier and repair company. I found my first work mentor, Amy, who took me under her wing and served as a mama when mine was hours away. She was amazing at guiding me and teaching me how to really make it on my own after college. I'm sure I ended up disappointing her in my stint there, though, because I didn't know how to keep my hands to myself.

Just like how I studied nonstop at the music store to know everything I could, I did the same with printers. I took home every manual they had because I wanted to be a knowledgeable resource on every single part. I wanted to help the customers as much as the technicians and the only way to do that was with knowledge of the product, problems, and solutions.

However, this wasn't a women-only business, so of course I got distracted playing with the men. One man was married and twenty years older than me, more than likely going through a midlife crisis. He had the same height, build, and look as Jon Hamm, who may still be one of my biggest celebrity crushes. We'd sit next to each other to work, but we'd let our arms gently rub, or our legs and feet touch under the table. We'd laugh and flirt, and lean in and whisper things. We ate it up, despite how inappropriate it was.

Then came one of the technicians who regularly hung around my office. He was a little shy, but equally bold in the most surprising ways. We started texting and hanging out. Those hangouts eventually turned into more. Oh, and I should mention that he was also engaged to the boss's daughter. To be fair, I didn't realize that for the first three months because no one ever mentioned it. By the time I found out he was in a relationship, we had already started making out. So once I knew, we tried to be good for as long as we could while still hanging out as though that was going to last long. He'd share his predicament by dedicating songs like "Lips of an Angel" by Hinder to me on the radio. *Wait... a boy who is actually dedicating songs to me? I didn't have to pretend and make it up like I did for the high school newspaper?* Yep, he found another one of my soft spots, so eventually we both gave in to the temptation.

The boss ended up walking into my office and quietly shutting the door one day after about six months of the affair. We were busted. Apparently they had been monitoring our emails and he told me that it needed to stop. Not only was it inappropriate, but because that was his daughter's fiancé. The environment got a bit more awkward in the office until I quit.

The only reason I finally quit is because my brother Isaac, who was only twenty-eight at the time, nearly died. He was at work, when he suddenly got light-headed and had to sit down. Thank God someone recognized he didn't look good, because they called the paramedics who arrived seconds before it would have been too late. Since then, his heart has relied entirely on a pacemaker, with more conditions diagnosed with age.

Once I got the call, it suddenly felt like I *had* to be back in Central Illinois to be closer to family. But I think my clock in Michigan had simply expired, because I didn't stay long in Central Illinois either. I soon moved again, this time closer to Chicago to start my master's degree in counseling. After six months of classes, though, I lost faith in my ability to be able to provide family counseling and still be upbeat and happy going home to my own family someday. So, I switched to an MBA in Human Resources instead, making another move to Wausau, Wisconsin as I chased yet another man.

I rarely stayed a year wherever I went, whether in a place or job. There was always some reason to go, and I'd find it no matter what. As soon as I got settled, I was ready to leave. That's still in me, although fading a little bit—now I have kids to think about, too. I thought this type of impulsivity was a bad thing, but the thing is... it's what I *needed* to do on some level, I just did it with the wrong things guiding me. Usually because of some man.

The dream I had when I was younger to go to different countries and immerse myself in the culture, the people, and write about it all, was given to me for a reason. That dream was birthed out of the gifts God had granted me and desires He already put on my heart. He gave me the ability to adapt to new environments quickly so I could make this dream happen.

So internally, I still had the intuitive *feelings* of what I was supposed to do, but the way I acted on them wasn't the original plan. I never followed through with that dream to travel and write. What would have been a pure compass guiding me, I tainted with the other reasons to keep me moving instead, usually pointing to a boy who wasn't truly worth my time.

I felt like I was messing up my life with these random moves, but I didn't know what else to do with the urge. Randomly going here and there for all the wrong reasons. I can barely even remember the men I lived with or the houses I abandoned. For example, I briefly moved in with a woman who was training to be in fitness competitions and it was *intense*; regimented eating schedule, certain foods banned from the house, egg yolk everywhere. I bounced out of there within weeks without letting her know or paying. I can't even tell you what city this was in because I moved so much.

I sold and repurchased things so many times that I probably could have been a millionaire if I didn't hit reset as many times as I did.

I see this happening with so many people. We have this zeal, passion, interest, reasons for our innate traits—but how we apply them is misguided. We miss the mark and make a mess of our lives when we don't trust the dreams we've been given. Instead, we are turning left when we should have turned right; we are going south when we should have headed north. In my case, I stayed in the U.S. when I could have been in a different country. If we don't apply our gifts to our dreams, we get lost.

I've always considered myself an intuitive person, but it took me a long time to trust my inner voice. Even today, I have to fight doubts about whether it's really God's voice I'm hearing, because my past wants to infuse doubt in my future.

Two things have changed that. One, I now ask God what step I should take instead of just leaping. Two, recently I've learned what a God echo is. When we think we hear His voice once, all we have to do is just open our eyes and ears, and if we heard what we thought, we'll hear or see it in another way. That's the only confirmation I need these days to keep moving forward in the direction I feel called in.

I have no doubt that if I understood God's voice more back in the day, I would have packed up my things and traveled to the countries I was supposed to visit. I would have done more and seen more than what I have today. I would have twenty books already out and published. And as much as I wish I had gone a different route sometimes, I don't doubt that the possibility is in my future still.

Nonetheless, I was doing a lot of learning, even in the midst of taking the wrong turns, and that's what was counting the most. With the way my life has been unfolding lately, I have no doubt I'm where I'm supposed to be, which tells me that it can all still work out as God intended. God continues to refine me with every step I take, and I know more than ever that I'm truly guided, and not as impulsive as I once considered myself to be.

strong, not fragile

I'VE ALWAYS HAD A DESIRE TO BE STRONG—PHYSICALLY, mentally, emotionally, and spiritually. My first tattoo says STRENGTH with Philippians 4:13 under it: *I can do all things through Christ who strengthens me.*

One of my favorite stress-relieving activities used to be boxing. I had a punching bag set up in my garage, and would go out for thirty minutes to punch and kick that thing while listening to "Last Train Home" by the Lostprophets, "The Quiet Things That No One Ever Knows" by Brand New, and "Headstrong" by Trapt on repeat. Using my arms like that always makes me feel the best.

I was a waitress in high school, a job I loved because it allowed me to talk to customers in a very touch-and-go fashion. There wasn't any commitment needed so I could always show up as a happy, high-vibing version of myself. Customers called me Smiley, so my co-workers started calling me that, too. I smile all the time, even if I'm not happy, because it's that people-pleasing bit in me. *Let's always make other people feel comfortable, so smile and be nice and pretend everything is okay.* No one ever really knew what was behind the smile.

At my first job after college, they also called me Smiley. It was

pretty cool to see a nickname transfer to a completely different physical location without prompting. It was that echo in a sense. Apparently it's what people used to see in me: my smile, above all else.

However, right before I moved back to Illinois, in my apartment
in Michigan, I'd spend time in front of the mirror, working on how
not to smile. Something finally cracked me while I was there.
Perhaps it was guilt sinking in about my role in every situation with
a man that crossed the line. Maybe it was being on my own and
living alone so far from home. But I suddenly realized that smiling
as often as I did was too inviting. It gave men the impression they
could get close to me. It made people think I was different from
what I was. It made me appear good when I felt anything but that.

I remember setting out to the grocery store purposefully with a
scowl on my face, acting tough, acting alert, acting like I was
prepared to defend myself if anyone ever tried anything with me.
When I caught myself smiling, I'd replace it. I stopped talking to
people as freely. I kept to myself more.

It was the last time anyone ever called me Smiley.

A couple years later, in one of my first corporate jobs as a development training agency assistant in a well-known insurance
company, I encountered the "mean girls" of the corporate world. I
foolishly assumed those only existed in high school. Nope, still here.
And it wasn't my last encounter with a group of girls who believed
themselves better than everyone else and created lies about anyone
who threatened a future promotion.

Unfortunately in this particular group, the manager of our little
division was also a member. She and I never hit it off; I'm not even
sure why she hired me, although I assume the decision came from
someone above her.

I was more reserved than the others and more of a processor
than someone who raised their hand and shared their thoughts with
the group. To this day, I'm still like this—more likely to ruminate
on what was discussed and then share ideas one on one rather than
interrupt someone else in a group setting. I sit back and let other
people speak first.

But, since I wasn't doing things like everyone else, I was singled out. The manager took me into her office one day and threatened to fire me. She went on a rant saying I'm not a team player and that I'm the outcast and have ruined what was a tight knit group. I sat there, listening to her, unable to speak because when I get upset, I cry. If I get mad, I cry. If I get frustrated, I cry. That disconnect between my brain and my mouth gets severed when I feel big emotions. I lose my ability to say what I feel despite the thoughts in my head running wild and strong

I hated that I couldn't control my emotions as the tears trailed down my cheeks. Once I finally got my mouth to form words, I told her I disagreed and gave her multiple reasons. I reminded her of all the times I stepped up to help. I just wasn't doing it during conference room meetings; I waited until afterward.

Her response? In the most snarky tone ever, she replied, "Well, perception is reality, and this is how I and everyone else perceive you. So whatever you think is wrong."

I left her office and cried in a supply closet for a good thirty minutes. I could barely lift my head for weeks. I felt so much shame, embarrassment, and confusion. *How could anyone possibly feel that way when I have such a strong desire to help people?* But she told me *her* perception was reality and intentions and methods didn't matter. I felt misunderstood and started doubting who I was, constantly paranoid about how I was being perceived.

I believed something was wrong with me, when I should have realized how wrong *she* was. What she should have done was encourage me to speak up during meetings and coached me on some ways to do that despite being reserved. A good leader would not have ripped me apart.

Months later, we had to take the Myers-Briggs Type Indicator (MBTI) personality assessment for a professional development class. When I received my results, I felt validated. I hung them up on the outside of my cubicle as though saying, *"Look! This is me. This is why I act differently than you."* INFJ tendencies (introversion, intuition, feeling, and judging) showed up in all of my behaviors and my manager couldn't recognize them. I was "different" than the others and instead of honoring my unique strengths, she wanted me to conform to *them*.

And for a moment, I really considered that I had to be just like them and couldn't be who I was. I wasn't strong enough yet to know the difference.

But as the years have passed, this situation and a few others, shaped a passion in me when it comes to our unique strengths. It increased my love for human resources development, which I did for twelve years prior to starting my own business. I became passionate about helping managers recognize the individual strengths of their team and to stop stressing their weaknesses. Instead of focusing on why they aren't at the same level as other people or fit in the box, focus on what they do right with their unique gifts, natural tendencies, knowledge, and experiences.

Although I'm still working on holding the tears at bay when I'm mad, frustrated, or upset, I no longer put myself in a position of being treated as "less than" just because I'm not recognized for who I am.

As I mentioned, I don't have many clear memories from my childhood, but one that is the clearest is when I was taken to a church in Bernie and had to attend the kid's service. There was a short play being put on by the youth pastor, whose name I somehow *still* remember (Stan), about David overcoming Goliath with a slingshot. That scene absolutely captivated me and it will come to mind at the most random times. I didn't fully understand it when I was younger, but as I've gotten older, I've seen how we all face different types of goliaths day in and day out. It may have been the most memorable goliath that David killed, but it wasn't his last.

I've had memorable goliaths as well, and victory is always worth celebrating, but I know that just because I've defeated one, it doesn't mean the coast is clear. It just makes me stronger and gives me more confidence every time one of my goliaths goes down.

I'm constantly working on being stronger in every way possible. It's a work in progress. Sometimes I slide but I constantly learn new exercises and put myself in new situations. They don't always go as expected, but the steps forward push me to the next level. I've had a lot of those over the past few years, and even if they take me down momentarily, I will always rise because my determination to be stronger than I was yesterday always wins.

human, not perfect

THERE ARE ALL SORTS OF SCARLET LETTERS THAT CAN BE worn. Mine seems to be D. Divorcee. Most people in my life know I was married once before. Not many know that I was married *twice* before. I just don't think our marital status has to define us—maybe that's because I've always done it wrong.

I really struggled to write this because I feel like no matter what I say on the matter, someone will be hurt. But I think it's important to admit what's difficult because that's partly the purpose of my memoir—to shed light on what it's like to share our stories. There are things I would do differently. Things I wish I did do differently. Because my actions have already hurt people, and that's the part I regret most.

I reflect back on my childhood and clearly see that I never had any dreams to get married. There's a reason why my best friend at the time wanted to play Barbies and I wanted to play Ninja Turtles. I didn't want the romance, I wanted the action.

Both engagements, I wanted to say no.

Both weddings, I wanted to run.

I didn't listen to the only clear voice in my head, the one that should have mattered the most.

During my first wedding, I got drunk off one swig of something in a bottle my sister-in-law passed me before the ceremony. Everything got hazy. I kissed my mom on the mouth while going in for a hug—we don't do that. I was so confused, so out of my mind, truly in an out-of-body state. I kept looking at the door, wondering how fast I could get out of there, but then thought about everyone who had traveled so far, sitting in the auditorium of the church, waiting for us.

I didn't realize it at the time, but it was literally my soul leaving my body, knowing that I didn't want to be married to him. I felt the same disconnect during sexual interactions with men I didn't want but felt pressured to quietly take it. That association felt extreme though. *Was it really all that bad? What else was there? What was I actually running from? He's a nice guy, it'll be fine. Isn't this what I wanted?*

We got divorced after two big things happened. The first was when he outright refused to support my author career by telling me I couldn't pursue it. The second was that I couldn't get him to spend time with me alone. He had two best friends who had been together since high school who were married, and he didn't know how to do anything without them. After begging him to spend New Year's Eve just the two of us for once, and his refusal, I knew I was done. I loved his friends, but it's a bit messed up that he wouldn't do anything alone with me. There was something deeper happening with him, and I could feel it. Then of course he ended up marrying the girl he was dating right before me, and things made sense.

When we got divorced, the shame was immense. I moved from Decatur to Peoria before eventually ending up in Bloomington. On every rental application, on every W2 form as I started a new job, I kept having to write down "Divorced." Changing my name was depressing. I was having to jump through a million hoops, proving over and over that I am who I say I am. It was easy to transition to someone else's last name two years prior, yet going back to the name that I had for twenty-five years was near impossible. Having to constantly flash my divorce decree paperwork in order to get my identity back was an awful feeling.

It also created chasms in friendships because I couldn't seem to relate to anyone else's marital or family status. I felt more alone than ever.

I got tired of being labeled as a divorcee. I wanted to redeem that status. I wanted to be where every other woman my age seemed to be: happily married with kids. After dating two guys who were horrendous (including one who was abusive and stalked me for a full year, even following me on a work trip in Las Vegas), I was ready to change my life.

When I met my second husband, it was at the time where *all I wanted* was to erase my past. I was desperate. I had my eyes focused on being married, settled, and starting a family. He was stable, nice, and I knew he'd be a good dad.

I definitely manipulated that relationship early on. I told him I loved him earlier than I did. I convinced him we should move in together. I even pressured him about our engagement.

It may seem strange, but when I thought about marriage, I hadn't thought of it as having a partner who I could *enjoy* for the rest of my life. I wasn't focused on having someone who could be my best friend as well as a lover. I wanted a home with a family. I wanted kids. I wanted someone who would be a good dad to them. I wanted safety in loving and being loved, and I wanted to have some sort of control in it all.

When he promised me he would support my writing career after I told him my first husband wouldn't, I was in. That's all it took. It was such a significant moment for me. I remember exactly how I was sitting on the floor in my bedroom as we chatted on the phone. I remember muting him to squeal out loud as he *promised* that he would support me while I wrote books.

That promise is what I held on to every time I wanted to leave. Even on one drunken night when he yelled at me and told me no one loved me, that I had no friends, that I was pathetic, and no one wanted to be around me... I stayed.

I wanted that promise he made me, and I was scared I wouldn't get it again. He had tapped into one of the deepest parts of my soul that outweighed any other desire or common sense. I wanted to have the time and space to be an author as much as I wanted kids, and he gave me the dream that someone would support me while I did both.

When he proposed, "no" screamed in my mind. In fact, it echoed for about two days after as I debated whether I could take my word back. The writing promise kept me glued to him, though. I ended up turning my attention to my ring, creating a weird obsession with it. I'm not a jewelry person, so that should have been my first clue. It wasn't a big or super expensive ring, but it was modest and perfect. I loved that ring. I also loved his ring. When things were crappy between us, I'd always think, *but look at our perfect rings.* I don't have an explanation for that at all. I suppose it gave me something else to focus on in order to keep my attention off us. I should have cared more about us as a couple—as people—than I did about those rings.

We had happy times, don't get me wrong, but I believe we both knew deep down that we weren't supposed to be together. I really don't believe he loved the parts of me that were truly me, but he loved that I was good enough; and I felt the same way. I never truly loved him for who he was because I'm not sure I ever actually *learned* who he was. We were good enough. But good enough isn't the person you should be spending the rest of your life with.

We actually called off the wedding a couple months before our wedding date. We were in our bedroom in his townhouse after a fight. I sat on the bed while he paced the room. The moment we agreed to call it off, I swear both of us felt momentarily relieved. I remember the glimmer of light shining in his blue eyes again. We fought all the time and it was wearing us both down.

After a few hours, though, we realized we had to call our families and let them know—our families who already invested much time and money into our wedding planning. *They would be so disappointed.* Well, except my brother Isaac, who already declared he wasn't coming to the wedding and wasn't letting my sister-in-law, who once was one of my best friends, be my bridesmaid. He was pissed at me for getting divorced the first time, so he refused to come to my second wedding. I was angry at him for years for his lack of support. Now all I can do is chuckle about it because Isaac could see what I couldn't: I shouldn't have been getting married again.

During our short-lived wedding pause, I thought of his mom, especially, who was thrilled to see her youngest son get married. He, too, thought of his mom, who floated a large part of the bill since my parents couldn't put much into it after paying for my first wedding. I also thought about how much of a pain in the ass it would be to move out of his place when I had just sold my town-home, and how I didn't have money to move again. So, to not disappoint people and complicate things, we eventually came to the conclusion to go through with the wedding.

It's hard to sum up why a marriage ends because it's always so layered, so I won't try here. But the promise he made, that I held to like superglue, was a moot point when it came time to cash it in. It took far too many arguments to uphold the integrity of that promise. Which was followed by constant guilt trips held over my head.

When we hit year five, still on the rocks, he started ending our arguments with, "We might as well get divorced." He took our arguments to the extreme, and it would drive me nuts. By the sixth time I heard him say it, it was looking more apparent that this was the only option that would end this cycle of suffocation and exhaustion between us.

I found myself thinking, *If this one ends, I'm never getting married again.* At first, the thought shocked me, but then, after a few times of me admitting it out loud to friends, I realized there was actually something liberating about the idea.

I eventually asked myself, *Wait, why am I so settled on never getting married again? Is it because maybe, just maybe... I never wanted to get married in the first place?*

With the permission I gave myself to explore that idea, there was a resounding *whooooooosh*... the release of an expectation I no longer had to strive for. It gave me pause to explore my beliefs. Maybe marriage wasn't something I wanted... *and maybe that was okay.* I wanted kids; the husband felt more like a required part of the package deal versus a choice I was making.

I was terrified to tell my family and friends we were separating (which is just a much easier way to drop the news, even though a divorce was clearly imminent). I didn't want to deal with the push-back, the drama, when for once in my life, I felt so damn confident, and a little bit guilty, but mostly excited about this revelation of simply not being a marriage type of gal.

The majority of loved ones took the separation well enough. Including my mom, which surprised me.

But the part no one took well? When I said I didn't want to get married again at all. That perhaps marriage was never for me, and I see that now. That all I wanted was kids.

Now, that... *that* was the end of the world. That was unacceptable. There was *no* way I could *not* want to be married—that was completely unnatural.

This is what I've come to realize: Saying you don't want to be married is a death wish to some people because they hear you don't want to ever be loved. To them, you're conceding yourself to a sad life of loneliness and failure. You're going to die alone with twenty-five cats eating your rotting body.

But I had to realize on my own that it's okay to shatter other's expectations. I don't believe marriage has to be the end-all, like they don't believe that singlehood should be the end-all.

My mom sent me a text a week after I told her and said something to the effect of, "This just isn't what I had ever dreamt of for your life." I was stunned to receive the message. Here I was, with two incredible children, running a beautiful business after success in the corporate world, living my dream of writing and publishing books, a master's degree, and overall, a very good life. *However...* just because I didn't want to be married, suddenly her vision for my life had crumbled.

I know this is a bit of an exaggeration on her end, fueled more by shock than anything else... but why does it feel like out of all the things a woman can do in life, being married is touted as the best? I don't feel like men have the same expectations put on them. They're expected to succeed at their job; women are expected to succeed in getting married and having kids. And I played into that, thinking that just because a "good enough man" wanted to marry me, it was a victory.

When I first announced the divorce, I played the enemy. *It's on me. I'll take fault. I'll let him take whatever he wants to have*—the hardest being the house. I felt bad. I felt guilty. I thought I was being the bigger person.

It took about eight months to realize how incredibly wrong that way of thinking was.

I wasn't the guilty one; I was the brave one. I was the one who finally made the call. All the times he would say, "So we should just get a divorce, huh?" He wouldn't have taken it there if he didn't truly want it. The final fight we had, I replied, "Yes, I think we should." Suddenly, he retracted his statement like he didn't suggest it because he didn't want to be the one who said it first. He wanted to be conscious-free. But the thing is... he knew it, too: we didn't belong together.

I desperately miss the idea of the family unit being all under the same roof, but I never miss him. As harsh as that sounds, it's the truth, which confirms everything I always knew deep inside my gut. I would be really surprised if he missed me as opposed to the idea of me or a warm body next to him. He never told me he missed me, and he definitely never fought for me, and perhaps there's no reason he should have.

Time has passed and I keep growing and evolving and learning about myself, as well as more of what God wants for me, which has significantly changed my life. I've given myself grace to understand that I'm a work in progress and my feelings on this subject can change.

I went through a full year of believing I didn't want to be married. I had to allow myself to be able to say it and live it. It gave me a sense of freedom, of ownership after feeling like the past few years were out of my control. I needed to be able to test out a new identity. I needed to be able to say I didn't need something we are conditioned to want.

But as the pain subsided, as I've reconnected with my true self, I've realized more of what my mom and other people in my life were shocked to hear. Of course I want to find someone to spend my life with. I still struggle with the idea of entering another marriage because of my experiences. I'm terrified of feeling "trapped" with someone again and absolutely refuse to go through another divorce. But I know without a doubt that I want to find the *right* person to experience this life side-by-side with. A true partner. And I have a feeling that when I finally find him, marriage may seem like the most obvious way to honor our love and our family, and that makes me look forward to that day.

original, not fake

WHEN I WAS YOUNGER, AROUND 1999-2003, LIVEJOURNAL and DeadJournal (the latter for the more angst-ridden teens, and I wavered between both) were used to share my deepest thoughts, putting them out into the void for whoever to stumble across and read. What I loved about those platforms is that we weren't sitting around in anticipation for pings on our phone, hoping we would get likes and comments on our posts. None of that mattered back then. We just put out our deepest thoughts into the world, feeling the release that comes from sharing who we are and standing boldly behind our words. We owned our voices, not trying to cater them to someone else's expectations. We wrote individual manifestos and supported each other in our perspectives and beliefs, encouraging each other to keep sharing and being vulnerable.

One of the best compliments a writer can give another writer is, "Man, I wish I wrote that," whether it's the *way* they wrote something, or the idea, scene, or book itself. I've expressed this to a few clients of mine throughout the years, and I always wonder if they understand the depth of that compliment, or if it'll click only after they've been in this author business for a few more years.

While in sixth grade, I fell in love with Richard Marx's "When I See You Smile." Oh how I wanted a boy to dedicate that song to me.

I sang it to myself all the time. I wrote down the lyrics in one of my notebooks, changed a couple of lines, and would show it to people and say, "I wrote this." I don't remember if I called it a poem or song, but I roll my eyes now because I'm sure people recognized the song. It was so good that *I* wanted to be the creator of it.

I was lucky enough to score Mr. Reliford as a teacher in seventh grade and he quickly became a favorite. He saw me through some of my worst moments. I was really starting to spiral into the darkness around that time. *The Chicken Soup for the Soul* books were popular, and I picked up an edition either in his classroom or from my mom's collection. There was a powerfully-written anonymous poem by someone who had lost a friend in a drunk driving accident. I made up some story about how I was the one who wrote it, that I was the one who recently lost a friend, and showed it to him.

It's hard to connect with my motivation behind such a lie. I think either I really wanted attention, a male's affirmation, validation that I was a good writer (even though it wasn't my writing), or I was using it as an excuse to try to get out of something. Or maybe it was just yet another crazy story that I let run in my head as I made things up left and right during that time period. I could tell in Mr. Reliford's eyes he knew I didn't write it. He remained kind and steadfast, though, when anyone else would have called me out on the spot. It wasn't the last lie I told that year. I was lost, and he knew that, so he provided a listening ear.

I always knew I wanted to write something great. All writers do. We'll never usually know when we do write something great, though—or at least not in a way that ends up truly landing with the masses.

Usually we end up thinking everything we write is crap and we'll want to rewrite it a million times or toss it completely.

The Last Look is one of my favorite books I've written to date. It means the most to me because it felt like my soul wrote it, not my hands. There's a scene where the main character, Haleigh, finds out that someone passes away (I can't reveal too much without spoiling it). The way that whole scene unfolds is one of the absolute best pieces I've ever written. I've probably re-written every other paragraph in that book a million times but that scene is still the original. I sobbed while writing it at 3:00 a.m., as I tried to squeeze in my self-imposed writing quota for the day while juggling a newborn baby and toddler who would both wake frequently.

One the best parts about writing fiction is how we can weave in pieces of reality, and it becomes as therapeutic as say... writing a memoir. I got into writing women's fiction after struggling with my marriages. There is no doubt that those who read those books after reading this memoir will catch scenes I've shared in not-so-subtle ways. Knowing this truth as an author, when I read any other author's fiction piece, I'm always wondering, *Which part of this actually came from their real life?* It's like dissecting Taylor Swift's lyrics and trying to figure out who she wrote about and what happened.

What I love the most about using our life experiences and turning people we know into characters is that it makes our writing original to us. It also ends up meaning more than anything we pull solely from our imagination.

We're in an age where AI is increasingly popular and people are wondering if it will take over real human writing. I'm convinced it never will. Not for as long as we want real emotions to be infused into our writing. I have worked with experts in AI, trying to figure out some way to use AI to make writing easier and faster. I think it's a fantastic brainstorming tool to help generate ideas since it emulates a conversation with another person and that one idea can lead to another until the right idea lands. But I've tried all the different recommended prompts to get AI tools to write books like I would or like any of my authors would and it fails every time. It may sound good to the author at first because it's a more eloquent writing style than their own and usually with some poetic spin. However, if they take a step back and be less critical of their talents, they can see that their words are always better.

I've had clients use AI in their writing, and I can *always* tell. It flattens the unique story details, special phrases the author uses, and writing style. Unlike Mr. Reliford did with me, I actually call my authors out when they try to pass it off as their own writing because I don't want them to lose sight of how wonderful their real voice is.

I was also a kid who had no sense of the value I brought or the uniqueness I carried when I did the things I did. It breaks my heart when I see adults willing to surrender to the same doubts about themselves. Writing should always be reflective of who we are. Readers should be able to read someone's book and then meet the author in person, and it feel like the same person they've already come to know in reading their book. But when we authors are constantly obsessing about writing like someone else or sounding like someone else or comparing our book to someone else's, we miss out on the magic of our personal impact.

I've come to see that it's usually the crappiest of situations, whether actions we take or things that happen to us, that unveil our mission and purpose.

For me, my purpose was uncovered through the mistakes I've made, which stirred my unyielding passion to honor the authenticity of a person's voice, give them a place for their voice to be heard, and to capture the truth of their stories. There will never be something more appealing than an actual human sharing how they are feeling, thinking, experiencing life, or seeing the world in their own words, whatever form it takes. A life where we cannot express ourselves in our most original form is not a life I want to live.

The truth is, at some point, whatever platform we use for self expression will go away, like those online LiveJournal and Dead-Journal entries I wrote a long time ago. Blog articles will disappear. Social media will forever change. But a book, once published, has true staying power. It is the *most* powerful way to share the messages of our hearts because it's intimate and timeless. It's why I'm such an advocate for making sure the books we write truly reflect us, and not someone we're pretending to be. It becomes a mark that we have forever left on the world and permanently showcases who we were.

loved, not unlovable

ONE THING I'VE NOTICED RECENTLY IS THAT I CATCH myself paying close attention to interactions within marriages and families. The families that seem like they're enjoying every minute together and are affectionate with each other. The marriages that have been together for decades and they operate as one, but still keep their individual identities.

I'm now in a community where I'm surrounded by healthy examples of marital and familial relationships. Not ones trying to sweep things under the rug; they're actually operating in the authentic truth of all sides of who they are, and not just the positive, public-facing aspects. They'll be real about the struggles but also be real about their love for each other.

I wish I had more of this surrounding me before I entered into the relationships I did. I wish I noticed how strong relationships truly operate. I should have been learning from them.

My favorite moments are when these couples are in conversation and they're facing each other directly, not looking at others, not doing it just for show; they're completely engrossed in what each person is saying, their eyes darting from their significant other's eyes down to their lips and back.

I take note and melt.

Conversations with my ex-husband did not include looking at each other, but instead, usually staring at some electronic device. If I asked him a question, he would respond but he'd regularly trail off in half of the sentence as though he could no longer give me his time or energy. It's as though he was doing *just* enough to check the box, "I responded." But did the response count if half of it was barely spoken and the whole exchange just seemed like it made him miserable?

Too many times to count, he'd leave the room or go into the garage as the door would shut between us as though I wasn't just in the middle of saying something.

That was how I was spoken to for eight years by the person I was with the most, and the person who should have cared the most about what I was thinking and feeling. It repeatedly fed into the already-existing narrative that no one cared about what I had to say. It's why I often rush through what I want to say when I'm talking to someone and leave out the majority of it. I feel like I don't deserve to take up space.

It's not all his fault; I brought a lot of unrecognized trauma and emotions to the relationship that I hadn't properly dealt with. I didn't stand up for what I was worth because I had yet to recognize my value. I didn't demand that his attention go to me because I was hoping it would automatically, and so I allowed each encounter to play into the narrative of what I already expected.

Maybe that's why, in a strange way, I found comfort in our relationship early on. He reminded me a lot of my dad. He represented what I was used to. Deep down, I wanted more, but what I believed I deserved was met spot-on.

Until I woke up and realized... *I'm actually worthy of being spoken to with full energy, interest, and love.*

Let me say that again...

I'm worthy of speaking and being listened to with full energy, interest, and love.

And not only when they expect something in return as though they deserve an award for having a real conversation with me.

There have been few relationships in my life, both romantic in nature as well as friendships, that felt based on true love. Most of my relationships have felt transactional, with conditions tethered to them. "I'll love you as long as you do..." or "I'll love you as long as you'll be..." or "I'll love you as long as you'll love me."

What about loving me no matter what?

The one thing that has grabbed my attention during romantic movies lately is the way the male character will fight for the female character once they think they've lost her. Oh, how that idea is drilled into our heads. Maybe for some women it happens.

The only time I was ever fought for was by Aaron when I was seventeen.

The men I'd get sucked up in were the ones who would buy me things. Gosh, the times I heard, "I've spent so much money on you!" as though I made them do it, is sickening. It was always held over my head, like they were buying me off until they were through with me. It wasn't ever a loss of *me*; it was a loss of the money they'd spent on me. It was the same thing when I got divorced and the first conversation was not, "I don't want to lose you!" but it was, "I'm not losing the house or the money."

So I talk myself into thinking it's a relief for them to be done with me because of the burden I must be. I also hold a belief that I'm a novelty at first, but wear off quickly. I hate to say it, but that is one I still carry with me today. I've come to realize I'm going to have to be friends with a man *before* a romantic relationship can grow.

I'm waiting for God to reveal to me who He wants me to be with. I believe one sign will be that it's someone who will actually fight for me, who will not want to let me go, who wants me part of his life and is willing to make sure that's exactly where I always stay.

It's such a hit to the ego to be perfectly honest. *Lord, show me the one man who will stay. Show me the one man who will actually pursue me. Show me the one man whose love for me will be unconditional.*

In the meantime, I have two young boys who regularly take a knee and propose with rings created from whatever craft item they can find, and I happily accept every time. They're little my Romeos and a constant reminder of what true love is.

With my kids, I'm intentional in reinforcing that no matter how much they act up, make bad choices, don't perform as "expected"— they're still loved and I'm proud of who they are. I want them to know that at the core of their being, outside of anything that they do or fail to do, they are wrapped in true unconditional love.

But I feel the pull every now and then, my automatic response to hold things over their head, to make it seem like they have to work for my acceptance or love.

I know this sounds harsh. Why would a parent operate that way? But so many of us do, in our parenting, our friendships, our relationships. A purposeful guilt trip when someone makes different choices than we want them to make. We take away things to punish them, such as toys when they're young, we withhold talking if it's a friend, we withhold sex in a romantic relationship. It's a manipulative, fear-based method of control even though we would avoid any connection with those words. These actions silently communicate, "You disappointed me, so I'm going to with-hold love from you until I feel like you're worthy of it again." The unfortunate outcome, though, is that it creates an environment where someone is unsafe to be themself.

At thirty-nine, as I shot my first gun ever and hit target after target, I waited for my dad to say, "Good job!" or, "Wow, you're really good at this!" When we went back into the house, he told my grandma that she was really good at hitting the small target, but had yet to compliment me. I was waiting for his confirmation as though I needed it to know I was good even though my actions clearly proved that I was.

So, silently to myself, I repeated the phrase, *I'm still loved. I'm still loved.* Only recently have I fully understood and accepted God's love for me. It's the one love I know is truly not based on what I do or don't do, and I don't have to wait for confirmation of it.

And deep down, I know that to be true of my dad's love of me as well. When I came back to visit my parents with my kids three weeks after I shot the gun with my dad, he told my boys, "Your mom is really great at hitting the target!" What I realized is, just because my dad may not always express it in the ways and time that I need it, I understand that he loves me no matter what, and I remind my little girl self that he's always felt that way about her, too. I simply perceived it differently for most of my life.

I can say that now because I see how my kids are experiencing big emotions at their young ages and they struggle with how to channel them. Some days they do and say things that stun me—I wonder how they could possibly behave like that. Whether outright lying to me, hitting me from frustration and anger, or saying, "You're the worst mom ever!" Of course, two hours later, my sweet boys will follow it up with about ten notes apologizing and saying I'm the best mom ever. No matter how much something may hurt in the moment, my love for them will never waiver. I don't stop loving them for a second. But it doesn't mean that they accurately perceive it. I may not always express my love in the way they need it, yet I'm always doing the best I can.

Just like I mess up with my kids even when I try my hardest not to, I know my mom and dad recognized their mistakes, even when they tried not to make them. I took certain things to heart as a little girl and created stories that were true based on my own perception, instead of their intentions. But as an adult, especially as a parent now, I see a new perspective from what I once believed to be true.

Two weeks after Easton, my first child, was born, I turned to my mom as she sat on the couch across from me.

"I'm so sorry for everything bad I ever did or said to you," I told her.

Because for the first time, I comprehended the capacity of her love for me and her need to keep me safe. Now every reaction she had and every word she said suddenly made sense. Fear of those we love getting hurt can make us want to hold on tighter and take control, but it doesn't make that love conditional.

I'm constantly doing things like my parents, things I said I would never do, and then having to correct myself. Sometimes it's hard to operate differently from the only thing you know. But my boys are tiny mirrors, constantly reflecting back to me every good move and every mistake I make.

Starting my business was both a blessing and a burden when it came to parenting. The way that the boys get to see me pour my passion into my job is a blessing. It shows them they can truly be whoever they want to be. Who would have thought that I could make a living as an author, book coach, ghostwriter, and publisher, wrapped up in stories and books every day? My goodness, my little girl self would be *so* proud this is her future.

The downside to my business is that there was a time that I let it overpower my priorities. I chose the emails, chose the phone calls, let the focus be on the business rather than my kids. I started the business during the COVID-19 pandemic, so they were home all the time, and I took advantage of that, just in the wrong way. I didn't appreciate those moments as I should have: a time to slow down and spend time as a family. I was teaching them that they come first—*unless* the business interrupts, and then they become second. That's not okay.

I tell them a hundred times a day how loved they are, not just by me, but by others in our family and by God. I remind them that they were made exactly as they were for a reason, so to never try to be anyone other than themselves. I want them to know they are loved and supported without conditions. But as much as I tell them, my actions need to back it up, too.

Part of Easton's creativity is his amazing storytelling ability. At his young age, though, sometimes half of what he says is a made-up story of something that happened, and not reality itself. Sometimes when I have a million things to do, it's really hard to sit and listen when I know that it's not even real, so it doesn't feel important.

But it's important to *him*. In his stories, he's trying to say something, he's trying to express a piece of him. And I know very well that, even though he's only eight now, there will come a day when he's not as interested in talking to me. So I want to soak up the moments he likes to talk endlessly now, because hopefully if I show him how important it is now for him to speak and be heard, he'll want to continue talking to me nonstop, even later in life.

One of the most important things I can do for my kids is make sure they are fully heard. That means putting down my phone, shutting down my computer, turning off the TV, turning down the music, and looking them straight in the eyes when they're speaking. Sometimes that means getting down on their level, bending to match their height. By removing distractions, I'm giving them the space to say what they need to say and all the time they need to say it, even if it takes them a while to get to the point. Because every word is important.

Besides, don't we all want to be heard?

I want my boys to find unconditional love not only from me, but from themselves within. Camden, ever since he was five, will pray, "Thank you, God, for Mom, Easton, Dad, and I thank you for me." I love that he will thank God for himself. I don't want him to seek external validation alone, because that'll always feel conditional if he doesn't know the truth within, above all else.

Those boys are my greatest accomplishments, my greatest joy, even in our hardest moments. I will spend every day of my life making sure they always know that they are fully loved no matter what.

And I know that I'm loved, too.

healed, not sick

THERE HAVE BEEN MANY TIMES I'VE FAKED BEING SICK OR hurt to get out of things.

I have faked sickness to get out of school.
Faked cramps or a hurt ankle to get out playing in soccer practices and games.
Faked passing out, for dramatic flair, when I found out that a guy I had given everything to was cheating on me—to the point an ambulance carried me away.
Faked having life-threatening illnesses to get people's attention.
Faked having the flu because I didn't want to go to different events or activities.

It's ironic I've faked being sick or hurt as many times as I have when getting truly sick is one of my biggest fears. These days, integrity is too important to me, and I no longer fake being sick. However, when I *was* actually sick, it wasn't a sickness I recognized for what it was when it was happening, despite how it was actually impeding my life.

The dark clouds of depression roll in faster than I can recognize that a storm is brewing. I've had to train myself to be alert to the little signals and stand guard. The depression is quick to take over my being, paralyzing me from my brain to my toes. I've had to literally grip the steering wheel as tightly as possible while driving to prevent my hands from turning my car into oncoming traffic, a wall, or off a cliff.

If I didn't have a relationship with Christ, I honestly don't know if I'd still be here. I wouldn't have bet on me. It's been God speaking to me every time in the moments that have threatened me, the Holy Spirit a roar slightly heard above the destructive storm. He's reminded me that those other voices whispering harmful things aren't me. Sometimes I have to scream over the voices, but I *know* they're not me.

One of the darkest depression periods lasted fifteen months and it was when I was pregnant with Camden. Yes, *while* I was pregnant with him, and then ten months postpartum. Hardly anyone talks about depression while pregnant, I sure as hell wasn't going to admit it. People were already telling me it was one of the happiest moments of my life and that I should be so grateful and to "just enjoy every minute"—but I wasn't happy. Not truly. And the guilt of not being happy just compounded my sadness.

It's not that I didn't want my boy because even to this day, that darn smile of his is what I look forward to seeing from the time I wake up to the time he falls asleep at night. He hugs me like he's holding on for dear life and gives the sweetest kisses where he gazes in my eyes afterward. The way he tells me he loves me out of the blue multiple times each day always makes me feel like this is what true love is. I love him with every ounce of me, as much as I love Easton. There is not a part of me that could fathom either one not being in my life. I'm crying as I write this because I don't ever want to be without them. One of my daily prayers is that they will both be holding my hands when I'm on my deathbed, telling me how much they loved having me as a mom.

Depression doesn't come with a warning. My episodes seemed to be triggered by hormones, especially as a deeply emotional person. Depression recognized I'm someone it could seize and control, so of course it knew I was even more vulnerable while pregnant and took the moment to infiltrate.

Once Camden was born, he didn't sleep at all for the first two years of his life. He'd sleep in forty-five minute spurts, at best. Throw a two-and-a-half-year-old on top of that, and it was *rough*.

The day before I was to leave the hospital after giving birth, my then husband told me he was going back to work the very next day. My mouth went dry and all I could muster was, "Really?" I was shocked, angry, and hurt. He had the option to stay home for a few more days, yet he was choosing to go back. *How did he not see I was going to need help?*

It felt like a punishment. Eight months after Easton was born, I had to fight to be a stay-at-home mom so I could also write. It was the promise he made when we dated, but now when it came time, he backtracked. We made a heck of a lot more money than the average couple, yet it still always came down to money as though we didn't have any. So when he announced that he was returning to work the day after I was to be released from the hospital, he was effectively saying, "Well, this is what you wanted, to stay home with the kids. Someone has to work, so figure it out."

There is truly no excuse for someone leaving their wife to care for a toddler and newborn she *just* birthed (and needed to recover from) when they have the time off available.

I was exhausted. I was scared. I was sad.

People who have never had postpartum depression don't realize how bad it really is because it's not something those who do have it want to talk about. It's everything that will make you feel like the absolute worst mother on this planet and a failure. As much as we don't want to say it, there aren't usually just thoughts about hurting ourselves, but thoughts about harming the very baby we gave birth to.

I don't want to admit it. I don't even want to write this. I don't want to publish this. Unfortunately, it's the truth and parents, current and future, and their support systems should be aware of it. If you know someone who has battled with depression, and then becomes pregnant, be cognizant and do a mental wellness check on them. We can't expect the normal answers about how blessed they are. Ask them to get real.

If someone came to me during this time, and asked how I was, I'd give my standard answer, "Things are good." But if they asked, "No, Lauren... how are you really?" looking directly in my eyes, I would have broken down and admitted everything. And I needed that.

But no one asked because everyone assumed everything was fine. I was far from fine.

Especially on days without sleep, on days when the crying would never end, on days when it felt like there was no support, no help, no way out. I had to fight against the thoughts telling me to cause harm to this innocent life form like I was in a combat zone.

I did one of the worst things: I stayed quiet. I didn't tell people I was struggling. I didn't get help. There's the societal expectation that I should be able to do it all, handle it all, and be filled with gratitude through it all because, that's just what moms do, so that's what I allowed to dictate my silence.

When I see those terrible stories about a mom going off the deep-end and killing her kids, my first thought is that she could have had postpartum depression that was never treated or healed and horrible voices telling her to do the unimaginable things. I know how quickly it can spiral—I nearly lost control of who I was. Someone new took over like I was possessed by a different spirit.

"This isn't you. This is separate from you."

If God's voice wasn't louder than the voices themselves, then Lord knows what would have happened. If I didn't have God, my entire world would have ended long ago.

For the first five years of Camden's life, I've carried deep guilt and shame related to that period. Sometimes I can see what I was feeling during the fifteen months of postpartum depression reflected in his personality. He's easily triggered and doesn't know how to control his anger (yet). He had nightmares often. He cried and whined over things he couldn't articulate. At four years old, he started doing a thing when he's upset: he'd shout, "You hate me! You hate me!" *Where in the world did he get this?* I can't help but think... *From me. That's where.* Early on, he sensed it.

How could it not affect him when everything in my body was feeding into and building his little body? I'm constantly trying to make sure he knows how important his life is. How much I love him. How incredible of a human being he is. I apologize to him all the time, although I'm not sure he knows why.

I'm sorry I had so many negative thoughts.
I'm sorry I had so much hate in me.
I'm sorry I was so miserable.
I'm sorry that I acted like I didn't want to be pregnant.
I'm sorry that I had to make you come into such an unwelcome environment.
You are important.
You are perfect exactly as you are.
I am so grateful for you.
I love every part of who you are.
You are going to do amazing things.
You are here for a purpose.
And I learn every single day from you.
You, my love, are perfect, wanted, and purposeful.

I will spend every day of my life making it up to him. I can't help it. Camden will know every single day how much he's loved and how I truly wanted him, even when I didn't realize it.

Postpartum is when I recognized my marriage wasn't going to survive. Maybe it was in part his immediate return to work, making me feel like I was on my own. Maybe all the times I tried to have real conversations with him that never went anywhere finally added up. Maybe I got tired of how he never seemed to believe I could do anything outside of typing on a computer without failing. But the part I remember the most was how I suddenly felt disgusting. We never had a relationship where we were completely comfortable with each other. If he walked into the bathroom while I was in the shower, he would say, "Sorry," and then make it seem like he couldn't look at me. I would get the worst migraines and ask him to rub my neck. He'd do so for about thirty seconds before he'd stop, like he couldn't stand to touch me.

It's one thing to endure this regularly, but when these things occurred during my postpartum depression, it had a profound impact. It took me down. For years since, I believed I was disgusting, because of how his actions and reactions made me feel.

In an attempt to take ownership, I took the blame. I didn't see it as a reflection of him, so I internalized every single reaction. *This is all me. There's something wrong with me.* So I got sicker mentally, emotionally, and physically. The depression grew. I ached all the time. I constantly felt sick to my stomach. My migraines increased.

I've done a lot of intentional work to figure out the source of my pain and heal what has been damaged. Even now, certain events shine a new light on things that I once thought had been healed, but it's a work in progress.

When the voices assert that I'm worthless, that no one loves me, that no one would know if I was suddenly gone one day, that I can't do the things other people do, and even the days that it feels like God is talking to everyone else except me... in those moments, I fall on the ground. I let my sobs overtake me and I say, "God, take it all. Take it all. Because I can't do it anymore."

I literally faceplant on the floor and melt into the ground when this happens. Like the creepy man at the Nashville Adventure Science Museum who shows what we would look like without bones, a slouchy blob. That's the way I feel. All the strength dissipates from my body.

The thing about being in those moments is this... it's okay to rest. That sudden atmospheric pressure that makes us want to drop to our knees, that's a deep desire to rest.

Many who have battled depression or suicidal thoughts feel like we're being bowled over by whatever it is we're facing. It's like crashing waves hitting us one after another, taking us under. The strength to stand is gone. The strength to fight is gone. Getting into a posture of complete surrender to God is the only thing that snaps me out of those moments. And guess what? It doesn't take a lot of effort to sink to the ground and surrender to the only one who can give me strength to get back up.

We have the chance to become different people today than what we were yesterday, but many times, it takes processing the past to be able to know what we need to do differently to become someone different. Writing is a beautiful exercise to help with that. It's not easy to sit here and dredge up the past, and many people are afraid to write about their past for that exact reason. This memoir has been the hardest thing I've ever written, especially when intentionally showcasing my most shameful moments. I've waded through a lot of muck to get to the truth and the real stories of who I am.

But it's important to understand that retelling the past isn't announcing that the past is who we are today. It's saying we experienced something and we're celebrating that we came out on the other side, and all that we learned as a result. It's about growth, resilience, and strength. For me, it's about when God pulled me out of darkness and gave me the greatest gifts (such as my children) in times of deep pain. And as I sit with my children and hold onto them, I'm grateful that I didn't give up on what this life could be, and I'm grateful for who I came to be because I kept fighting for one more day.

forgiven, not condemned

I WROTE THIS BLOG ENTRY IN 2021:

"Forgiveness creates expansion and room for greatness."

I read a book that suggested you should spend thirty minutes per day asking for divine guidance on who needs to be forgiven so you can release it. Since lately I feel like I'm wearing a corset because I can barely breathe with aches that shoot from my heart to my back, I figure this advice is coming at an important crossroads in my life. Divine timing. I'm listening, God.
I never focused on forgiveness before...
So here's thirty-seven years of it:

I forgive him for using me to explore.
I forgive her for abandoning me.
I forgive him for lying to me.
I forgive him for not telling me he loves me in the most crucial periods of my life.
I forgive them for ignoring me.

I forgive them for letting me watch the movie that scarred me.
I forgive him for leaving out the pictures that scarred me.
I forgive him for stalking me.
I forgive them for forgetting me at practice.
I forgive them for forgetting me at school.
I forgive them for talking bad about me and spreading lies at work.
I forgive him for threatening me.
I forgive her for threatening me.
I forgive him for slapping my ass as he rode by on a bike laughing.
I forgive him for doing nothing and staying quiet as the asshole rode by.
I forgive him for telling me I set him up for high expectations just to let him down and then forcing me into bed.
I forgive him for not telling me about the illness that could have affected me.
I forgive him for pointing a gun at her.
I forgive her for making it seem like I'll always be fat.
I forgive him for lying to me about what he did to her.
I forgive him for talking to her when he was with me.
I forgive him for leaving me drunken on a busy street in a city that wasn't mine.
I forgive her for listening to them over the truth she knew with me.
I forgive him for his lies that threw my company under the bus.
I forgive him for his lies of work he couldn't perform.
I forgive them for their curses they sent my way.
I forgive him for forcing me because that's my "role."
I forgive him for controlling everything he knew he could.
I forgive him for laughing like I can't do anything right.
I forgive him for assuming I don't know anything that falls outside the lines.
I forgive him for lying and stealing because he has yet to know the truth.
I forgive him for always making me feel like I'm a disappointment.
I forgive him for not touching me when I needed it the most.

I forgive him for making me feel gross when I was in need of love the most.

I forgive her for never talking to me about the things that should have kept me safe.

I forgive me for making fun of him.
I forgive me for stealing from them.
I forgive me for the times I said I hate them.
I forgive me for stealing from him.
I forgive me for ever putting him above everything else in my life.
I forgive me for not prioritizing my health.
I forgive me for snapping at them when it's not their fault.
I forgive me for forcing him to watch porn.
I forgive me for being a child addicted to porn.
I forgive me for being so mean to him when he was so good to me.
I forgive me for not calling them more.
I forgive me for lying about my happiness.
I forgive me for giving away my power so easily.
I forgive me for losing large amounts of money.
I forgive me for choosing other people over myself.
I forgive me for the bad partnerships.
I forgive me for saying I'm not good enough.
I forgive me for believing I'm not good enough.
I forgive me for rehoming them and making them feel less loved.
I forgive me for all the bad thoughts I had about me, C, and others during my depression.
I forgive me for staying silent every time I should have said no.
I forgive me for not understanding everything I wish I knew about why I feel certain ways about the things I can't do.
I forgive me for thinking I'm gross, ruined, and untouchable.
I forgive me for choosing men who want to take what they feel is theirs and letting them.
I forgive me for not seeing my worth for what it is.
I forgive me for not using my voice to stand stronger in what I didn't want.

I forgive me for falling in love too easily with the idea of things more than the reality.

I forgive me for becoming numb when I should have been feeling it all.

I forgive me for using her pictures as though they're my own.

I forgive me for how lost and broken I was and desperate for any attention I could get.

I forgive me for manipulating to get what I wanted.

I forgive me for never really knowing none of that wasn't what I really wanted.

I forgive me for not loving myself more throughout the years.

I forgive me for letting him control my beliefs.

I forgive me for passing up the songwriting opportunity.

I forgive me for cheating on the interview for the job.

I forgive me for telling him the stories that weren't true.

I forgive me for saying the poem and song were mine.

I forgive me for pretending things were better than they were.

I forgive me for not extending grace when I should.

I forgive me for all the times I didn't realize how good things were.

I forgive me for all the times I wanted to hide who I really am.

I forgive me for the bad decisions I made that I have yet to release.

I forgive me for all the times I was too scared to face the truth.

I forgive me for all the times I was too scared to exude the truth.

I forgive me for all the times I didn't follow through.

I forgive me for all the times I rushed and didn't do it right.

I forgive me for not owning and recognizing my truth.

I forgive me for forgetting that God belongs in me as well as around me, and that He's the only source of the love, prosperity, and guidance I'll ever need.

I forgive everyone and everything including myself, inside and out, in past and present.

I release it all now.

The healing I've seen in people as they write their memoirs is one of my favorite aspects of my job. (Okay, to be honest, I have a lot of favorite things.) There is so much courage in diving back into the cobweb-filled, dark corners of our lives to uncover things we shoved away. But memoir authors do it to bring light to them and give them a chance to live in our minds in a better way. I've had clients undergo years and years of therapy, journaling, and healing, which is why they come to the pages to finally start writing their story. Yet in writing their story to help others, a brand-new perspective is created. The changes in someone from beginning to end of the process are evident in how they present themselves with greater confidence, grace, and ease.

When I wrote this blog entry in 2021, I was at the start of my own healing journey. I realized there was a lot that I had been holding onto and it was affecting my entire being. It's impossible to go through this life and not be hurt by people. We think we move on, but many times, there are residual effects, serving as puppet strings controlling our actions, yet we can't determine the source with the strings all twisted.

The only way to move on and truly forgive people is by untangling the strings, identifying what actually needs to be forgiven and releasing it as a weight you carry through whatever method that looks like for you. For me, it's writing it and reading it out loud, then taking a deep breath to let it all go.

I was surprised as I re-read this list from 2021 because there were things I included that I'd nearly forgotten about since writing them down. Writing it all down allowed me to truly forgive and move on. It didn't mean the memory was gone forever, but they were no longer burdening me and taking up space where better things could live instead.

I spent far too much time expecting other people to come and confess what they did to me. I spent way too much time hoping people would see the light. I spent way too much time feeling guilty about things that I did. I spent way too much time giving energy to things that no longer served my present or future.

The best thing I could do was forgive myself and others, and give those events that happened a new label. I stored them away as part of my past journey, but did not allow them on my path ahead. I can't go back and change the past, but I can control how I view it moving forward, and that's an empowering truth.

driven, not crazy

It took me twelve years to write *The Remedy Files* from start to finish. Twelve years of suffocating under a brilliant idea, having a clear dream, and not doing a darn thing about it.

What finally fueled me were those two boys of mine.

My *why* for the importance of fulfilling my dreams was immediately defined when my boys were born. While I was pregnant with Easton, I started getting more serious about my dreams. I knew I wasn't doing what I was born to do and I hated the feeling of not stepping into my fullest potential. Writing books was everything to me, an outlet, and yet I was doing everything except that. I didn't want Easton to come into this life and not know his mom as what I truly was: an author.

I also had dreams of reading the books I'd written to him, books that would become his favorite, books that were reflective of what he loved. I wanted him to learn about life and all the lessons from my books instead of other books.

So I got focused, determined to make it happen. I had the ideas, I had the skill, I had the purpose, but I lacked the discipline.

It was the first step though, since apparently I couldn't finish a book in all those years on my own.

It took the birth of Camden to *really* kick me in the butt. Especially since Easton was two and a half years old by then and I *still* hadn't made as much progress as I wanted. It wasn't a great feeling to realize that.

But it was hard to get any energy to write when I was battling postpartum depression so severely and not sleeping on top of it. I felt like I was barely surviving. I thought I had plenty of excuses not to write in the past; now I had legitimate excuses.

Until the day of the triple breakdown, an event that served as a catalyst for getting my life back on track. I stood in the kitchen with Camden in my arms and three-year-old Easton looking up at me from the floor. These two kids rarely slept, and were hysterical—they couldn't seem to stop crying. We had been going at it for hours at this point, so I broke, and became hysterical as well.

After a few minutes spent standing there, not knowing what to do or how to stop it, and feeling the familiar waves of a panic attack coming on, I heard a voice clearly say, "These kids are a reflection of what's inside of you."

I knew the truth the moment I heard it and it shook me.

In that same moment, I took a deep breath with a long exhale, and the chaos subsided. They didn't stop crying right away, but I became calm enough to handle it.

I sat with that experience for a few days, trying to uncover what the voice meant exactly. I couldn't deny its accuracy, but how do I fix the chaos inside when I felt so sad and overwhelmed all the time? What could I do to change it so my boys didn't have to feel it, too?

The answer was easy. It was the same one that came to me from when I was a little girl trying to sort out big emotions then too: write.

Some people find journaling to be therapeutic; for me, that was never the case. I need stories. Stories are where I can somewhat regain control by owning the narrative. Even if I am writing a scene in which something terrible happens, I know I can still control how the character responds and grows as a result.

So I went on a writing binge. I wasn't sleeping anyway so instead of just sitting there, unable to sleep due to constant anxiety that one restless boy would soon wake up, I wrote. My fingers pounded on the laptop keyboard in every limited, free moment, day and night.

I finished five manuscripts in nine months.

By the time I finished, without even realizing it, I was out of my postpartum depression. I don't know at what point exactly it went away, but I felt noticeably free when all five books were completed.

Some of these manuscripts were stories I had already started; a couple were brand-new ideas from start to finish. All were between 80,000-120,000 words in length.

Keep in mind, these were rough drafts, not finished master-pieces. However, it was a big difference when my first book took twelve years to complete and my second one took thirty days. I became disciplined, spending time working out some sort of plot (even though I'm a pantser naturally) so I had a plan of what I was writing when I sat down to write. I started off aiming to write 500 words per day, but within a matter of weeks, I moved the needle to 5,000 words per day because 500 was hardly a challenge, and I wanted to keep pushing.

I proved to myself that I could write books, not just once, but as often as I wanted no matter what else was happening. For the first time in my life, writing became as important as I claimed it was for all those years. Except now I was actually showing it through my actions and how I spent my days.

The only thing that initially changed in my ability to succeed was that my *why* had shifted. I had a brand-new reason for doing things. And even though the circumstances I was in were the worst they had ever been, I got it done because I had the drive.

Although, it also made me really question what in the world I did with my life before I had kids. Holy cow, I should have had twenty books written when I was in my twenties!

The Remedy Files: Illusion was short-listed for an award. They invited me to a conference where the winners were to be announced. I won first place. It was my first real writing award since those blue ribbons for the Young Author Award back in grade school. This time, they handed me a beautiful (and quite heavy) glass trophy with my name inscribed on it and a check. I actually won money for something I wrote. That was such an incredible moment and an unforgettable feeling.

Afterward, with the trophy in hand, I FaceTimed the boys who were staying with my parents to share the news. I'll never forget the look on Easton's face. He was only four at the time, but he understood the magnitude of my achievement and was so excited for me. He spent six months afterward telling everyone at his school and everyone he came across that his mom won an award for one of her books. To this day, when he sees that book cover, he always says, "You won an award for that one." I love that it's etched into his brain.

As my path grew from not only writing books, but helping other people write as well, Easton was watching. He watched me write books constantly, which inspired him to write at least fifty short stories within a couple of years. As he watched me on Zoom meetings with clients, he began hosting his own (pretend) Zoom meetings. As he'd watch me record videos for my groups, he would take my phone and record his own motivational speeches, encouraging people to write their books. Those are some of my absolute favorite videos. Easton repeated what he had heard me say, but with his own unique spin. I've watched his confidence grow as he's pretended to be a leader, which has made him an actual leader. When we published his first real book, *The Butterfly Tree*, his school had him talk about his story at an assembly in front of the whole school. Despite being naturally reserved, now he brags that he's "spoken to 1,000 people and can do *anything*." He sees that his own ability is unlimited.

It's not lost on me that if I didn't see my boys as what they were (my *why* to do better, to be more of who I was made to be, and to fulfill those callings that had always been on my heart), Easton may not be on the path that he's on right now. Not so soon anyway. He's getting opportunities to do things and step out of his comfort zone to challenge himself that I didn't get until I was in my thirties. That, to me, is one of the best gifts a parent can provide a child: the ability to escalate both the clarity of their dreams and the belief that they can be reached.

It's funny that all of this escalated while I was pregnant with Camden and immediately following. Camden shows more signs of being a sports guy than a writer like Easton, but one of my favorite things about him is that he gives 100%, all he's got, to everything he does, both good and bad. I'm pretty sure he infused that spirit into me (and not the other way around despite me birthing him). He frequently reminds me of the importance of giving 100% to everything we do, because anything less is just a waste. I think I needed a little Camden in me to get me over that final hump.

It's another reason I can't imagine my life without those boys. Them becoming my *why* is what changed me, what changed my life into something completely unrecognizable from my life before them.

I have always had an intensity to succeed in the things that excite me, whether that's studying songs and albums when I worked at the music store, or reading printer manuals to be successful in my first real job post-college. But usually those things came at someone else's approval of my hard work. Working on my own dreams that felt like mine only made it more difficult to seize the drive when I needed it the most.

It's not only the *why* that became clear during that time with my kids, but also the reminder that our dreams are not our own; they're meant to help others as much as they are to help us. And sometimes, focusing on what can help other people will drive us to complete those dreams. Suddenly, we realize that they're bigger than us and can serve a much greater purpose.

Many people don't realize how hard it is to write a book until they actually sit down and try, especially a book that's pulled straight from their soul, whether in fiction or nonfiction. I always tell my clients they have to have a *why* that's big enough to change them—big enough to keep them motivated. I thought my dream of being an author was a big enough *why*, but clearly it wasn't, because it wasn't enough to shift my daily habits. My kids are what it took for me. That's when the *why* became unstoppable—*I* became unstoppable.

called, not swayed

IT WAS MARCH OF 2020, AND I WAS SICK WITH COVID for the second consecutive week at the start of the pandemic when everyone thought that you would die. I was quarantined in my bedroom, away from my kids, struggling to breathe, and wondering if I would wake up the next day, or if my time to leave this world had finally come. I felt lucky to even make it to that point in life, but I didn't want to miss my boys growing up. That kept me hanging on.

It really got me thinking... *How am I living life? Am I doing things that are making a difference? If I die today, did I truly make any sort of true impact in this world?*

And the big one... *How would I live if I got to do it differently?*

Well, that question got me. Instead of hitting a redo button on life, I realized I could at least hit the refresh button right now, where I currently was, and change my future.

Up until this point, Burning Soul Press was just a DBA (Doing Business As), so I could use it as a publishing imprint for my books. But I was starting to understand that the vision I had back when I was nine, about someone stuck in a glass box, dying to be seen and heard, well, there was something bigger behind it. It's how I got the name "Burning Soul" Press in the first place. Burning Soul Press needed to be something more. *I* needed to do more.

Once I published my books, I was asked by people to read their manuscripts and provide feedback. I realized I was actually quite good at coming up with new ideas that would help their books be better. I loved it. One of my early non-paying non-clients (since I was just helping people and not doing it for pay yet), was a six-time best-selling author and the book was *good*. However, as I read it, I came up with some additions that would make it *great*. She couldn't stop thanking me and I thought, *YES. This is what I want to do. This makes me happy.*

I made it official by filing for the EIN so Burning Soul Press could be launched as an LLC.

I finally talked myself into making a social media post as well. It was just a small one, nothing too big because I was scared about people's reactions. A day later, I had someone who I worked with in the past and admired very much reach out to me and ask me if I would *write her book for her.* That was something I never once considered. Ghostwriting held a negative connotation for me. *Wasn't it bad that other people are writing books for someone who is then taking the credit for it?*

However, once I listened to her powerful story, I was captivated. She expressed how she knew it was time for the story to be out in the world, but she simply didn't have the time, energy, or interest in fully writing it herself. When she asked if I would help, it was a resounding *yes*! I wanted to help her.

I just had to do a lot of research first, including what ghost-writers even got paid. It turned out, it was a lot of money for one project. I gave her a quote for $36,000. She said yes, she was in. Including the new members of a group book writing program I coached, I made close to $40,000 that first week of Burning Soul Press. God opened a new door and it was time for me to step through.

Burning Soul Press was officially launched, and I had no clue it was the end of the life I once knew, and a new one was just beginning.

If I thought writing my own book was hard, I was wrong. Ghostwriting was one of the most mentally taxing things I had ever done. Not only was there so much pressure to *want* to do good, but there were sudden expectations that this *would* be good. I had to step up and give it my all. As writers, most of the time, we're sure that our first twenty drafts are pure crap, but with ghostwriting, that same grace doesn't exist. We have to show up for the client and present what may have been our fifteenth draft as the first one, and stick by it with confidence.

Mentally taxing is one thing, but I wasn't prepared for how emotionally taxing it was. That shocked me above all. I was right there by her side, listening to every single detail of her experience, living it for the first time as she relived it. We cried together many times as we spent hours and hours on her story—I asked questions, she spoke, I recorded, and *then* I spent hours writing and rewriting, trying to get it right.

The experience surpassed anything I could have expected. It was beautiful and spiritual and wonderful on every level. Not only did she go through a transformation by having her story told in a new and lasting way, but I was forever changed, and once the book was published, other people were inspired, empowered, given light in their times of darkness...

I didn't want that feeling to end.

That's also when I realized the power in writing one's story, and even more, the way that power multiplies once it's shared with others. That's when this deep soul-driven desire to show every single person how important it is to capture their story became part of my life's mission.

It's interesting how people are so divided when it comes to both sharing intimate stories as well as ghostwriting other people's stories. We all have mental blocks for different reasons, and many times, we don't know the source outside of simply feeling the way we do. Why is the ability to open up and share who we truly are with the world—in whatever method—considered wrong? Is it because it makes some people feel uncomfortable?

My client and I discussed the concept of making others feel more comfortable several times when writing this particular book. We are hardwired, especially as women it seems, to create a comfortable environment for others, even if it means shrinking ourselves or sacrificing a piece of who we are in order to do so.

The sharing of true, deep, authentic stories is always going to feel extremely uncomfortable. The times my stomach has twisted in knots as I've written this memoir are too high to count. The times I've had to block out thoughts of certain people reading this for fear of what their reaction may be are too high to count. I feel like I have a million reasons to stop writing, all of which are fear-based, but there's only one that truly keeps me going: I feel convicted to share.

The conviction to share my story goes deeper than any level of discomfort that may arise in the process. I know sharing my story not only elevates the mission God placed on my heart, but also sparks connections with other people, and enriches the legacy I'm able to leave behind for my kids. This level of discomfort for myself and any it causes in others will eventually dissipate; the regret of never writing my story in the first place would last forever. I'm not willing to sacrifice what God has called me to do just to stay in a place of stagnant comfort.

Did I feel qualified to take on this client's ghostwriting project when she asked me? No. I doubted myself many times.

But I now realize God has a funny sense of humor when it comes to getting us to recognize our purpose, and it's always by giving us an opportunity that feels like it falls outside of our qualifications. He's waiting for us to take the challenge and trust that He's equipped us with what it takes. But it's up to us to say yes and take the leap of faith.

My entire life had been spent developing my listening skills, empathy, understanding, love for stories and reading, and writing abilities. I'm not sure what else I was waiting for to be "qualified." God had already qualified me a long time ago and He was the one handing over this job opportunity, so if He says I'm good enough, what is there to doubt?

I can tell you I wouldn't have done it if I knew how hard it was going to be; but I would do it fifty times over now knowing how my life has changed and how I've been positioned to impact the lives of other people as a result. I think sometimes that's why we don't always have a clear vision of where God is actually leading us. If we saw the full scope of the mountain we were being called to scale, we wouldn't do it. We wouldn't believe that we had the physical, mental, and emotional fortitude to survive; but He knows.

God has been calling me to write books since I was six years old. He gave me the mind to create stories, to write books, to process everything I was feeling in a very visual and emotionally effective, external way. For most of my life, I thought that was the dream I was pursuing.

I had no clue what the true dream actually was until I truly became an author and saw God's *full* purpose for me.

I'm convinced that God gives us all a dream, something that our limited-capacity minds can see and believe and get excited about; but the real vision surpasses that. The dream we see is the door, but the *real* target is what's behind it. If we saw the entire dream behind the door, we would doubt our abilities even more and never actually open the door itself. Already we throw out excuses and reasons for why we can't do what we've been called to do, and I just imagine God leaning up against the doorframe patiently saying, "You've got the key right in your hand, so why do you keep searching for it in all the wrong places? All you have to do is take the key I've given you, and open the door."

We like to make things so much more complicated than they actually are.

So now, when I hear people say they have a dream, my excitement is more for what's actually behind that door that's dressed like the dream they can see. I get giddy, *truly giddy*, at what's to come.

For me, my truth behind the door of being an author was being able to help other people write their life stories. I didn't even know I had a passion for memoirs in the way that I do today. I didn't even know I had this incredible gift to see how many books are in people's futures and to get the downloads that I get of what they need to write. There's no way I would have ever thought I'd be writing someone else's book for them and then go on to ghostwrite many others. I didn't even know book coaching could be an actual job that I could be paid to do. And I would have never thought I could be a publisher out of all things.

Over time, as my passion and interest became clearer, I started shifting the focus of Burning Soul Press to memoirs, inspirational, and self-help books because that's where the veil is pulled back and the rawness of each story is revealed.

My passion is refined. Who I am is defined. And I have a clear vision of my gifts and how I'm supposed to use them to serve this world.

It all started when I finally achieved my dream of writing and publishing my books. Once I did, it was clear God's true calling was yet to come.

growing, not stagnant

When I first started Burning Soul Press in a public fashion, I was ashamed to admit it. It originally wasn't supposed to be anything other than a side hustle, a way to make money while I was home with the boys.

Since I had the guilt over my head of now being a stay-at-home parent, I kept trying to find ways to make money without being forced to go back to the corporate world. I already went down the MLM route multiple times (from bags to hair products to crazy leggings) and even tried one that was a venture based on my own skills; designing little random downloadable guides and mini courses. I felt like people would think, "Oh boy, here she goes again."

So I didn't want to make a huge announcement. I remember trying to find the option on Facebook where you can post and ensure it doesn't reach people who actually know you.

As though selling to total strangers would be easier.

My theory was that I needed to prove myself with strangers before family and friends would approve of and support what I was doing.

Now, is that the actual reality? Absolutely not. That way of thinking is a bit skewed. However, many authors and entrepreneurs (authorpreneurs, because that's what they are whether they recognize it or not; the moment we publish a book, we're also now running a business) are terrified to have their family and friends know what they're about to do—because the ones closer to us will usually question *why* and ask *what*, creating more self-doubt, especially when more than likely, they're not going to understand it.

All I thought about were my five books I had released that were not *super* well done. I didn't invest in an editor and I rushed to put them out into the world, paranoid after my dystopian series that someone else would release a storyline *exactly* like mine. Even worse, I didn't market them. If a book doesn't get marketed, chances are that someone isn't going to accidentally discover it, considering the vast number of books that exist, despite how much we wish for it to be that easy.

As a result, I didn't want people looking up or reading my books and judging me for poor quality and lack of reviews.

"These crappy ones? No, thank you. There's no way I'm going to learn from her."

However, the real truth in it all? It's *because* I made so many mistakes in doing it by myself and *because* I failed over and over and over again, that I became damn good at what I do.

Those mistakes are also what fuel my passion to help as many other authors as I can. I can't even tell you the number of authors who want to rush, want to bypass important processes, want to get to the end zone without realizing that they're going to have major regrets if they continue that path. For the few who have ignored my advice, they then ask questions like, "Why isn't this happening the way I envisioned it?" *Well, because you didn't do it right and rushed the timeline, that's why.* Some people write a book wanting to hurry up and publish it, thinking it's the finish line, when really it's just a ribbon cutting, and the work is just beginning if they want to be successful. Trust me, I learned that very lesson the hard way.

It took a while to gain confidence in my failures and not let my pride stand in the way. I had to realize that those experiences helped me know the true right way to do things. There are similar companies led by people who brag about nailing everything perfectly with their first book and now they're showing everyone how to do it just like them. Honestly, it turns my stomach because firstly, not every system works the same for every writer because there are so many variables. And secondly, they're setting a completely unrealistic bar.

Perhaps I just appreciate failure in learning because it gave me the true behind-the-scenes knowledge and motivation I needed to keep going. The book industry is ever-changing and it won't always operate by the formula in your head.

When I once was so scared for people to see my failure, these days, I want people to challenge me on what I've done *and* what I know. I have real life experiences backing up my credibility with continual education to get better and better. I want to be the best I can be as an author, and serve my clients to the best of my ability, so they can be the best authors they can be as well.

There is *so much* imposter syndrome out there! Almost every single one of my clients face imposter syndrome at some point or another, even when writing their own life story. Yes, they'll question themselves as though they don't even have the authority or right to write about their own life. That's how deep these beliefs are for many of us, because it doesn't sound crazy in our head that we doubt we can write about our own lives.

We are so focused in our culture on degrees and titles and certifications, that we forget that life experiences carry just as much weight. Don't give me the person who has just learned about it through books, give me the person who has *lived* it and then spent some time learning so they can understand everything they went through better.

It's also why I tell future authors to take their time to ensure their book is done right: once you publish a book, you can't get it back. Even when I have now re-launched my old books, I can't ever take back the originals. They're sitting in people's homes and I can't sneak into each house and steal the old books back. The worst versions of my books will still get passed down from hand to hand without my knowledge or ability to control it.

A failure is only bad if we let it wipe us out. There will always be a negative consequence or emotion that comes from failure, but they're not meant to be permanent roadblocks.

One of my favorite quotes that completely changed my mindset came from Florence Scovel Shinn who said, "No man is your enemy, no man is your friend, every man is your teacher." Immediately, it challenged me to neutralize the emotional impact I've felt from every single person who has crossed my path, and ask, *What have I learned from this person or interaction?* Once I started this practice, I did it with experiences and events in my life as well. Even if I had a bad day, instead of getting upset, I'd ask, *Okay, what am I supposed to learn from this?* If someone hurts me, I ask, *What am I supposed to learn from them?* It resets the way I think about *everything*, failures included.

Bouncing back from my failures meant more trial and error, especially as I helped other authors write, finish, and publish their books. I didn't have to be perfect to do that; I just had to be at least one step ahead and able to guide them as we stepped from one rock to another across a bubbling stream, knowing they may slip, but holding their hand so they wouldn't fall.

Now, after helping hundreds of clients, I've learned that it's *because* I'm constantly seeking to grow and learn and apply what I learn, even if it means failing first, that makes me successful in helping them, despite the vast range of different individual goals, genres, and skill levels.

Burning Soul Press proved not to be the side hustle I originally intended; it turned into a full-fledged company quicker than I realized what was happening. I started being asked by other people if they could help out and be a part of it, and I was like, "Sure! Come on over. I could use the help!"

One may assume that after over a decade in the human resources field, that a person leading a company would know better than to randomly hire people in such a casual fashion. But I didn't expect to become an actual CEO with a full team, until it happened.

I was still operating very much from a people-pleasing mentality during this stage of life. I didn't know how to say no. I didn't know how to set boundaries. I didn't know how to protect the things God gave me, and that's the part that makes me the most sad about this particular phase. I was so quick to exchange pieces of my company, like I had been so quick to exchange pieces of myself throughout the years. I kept calling Burning Soul Press a true reflection of my heart, mind, and soul; unfortunately I wasn't treating any of those things with the care they deserved.

So, as the company grew and we needed more hands, I hired people who weren't only not the best fit for their roles, but also not the best fit for the company.

A startup is completely different from a corporation, and now, because of my experience making a small business survive over the past four years, I have way more respect for the corporate world than before. I think back to all the years we would waste hours in the day on the clock just chatting with each other, not realizing that someone is paying us to sit there, procrastinate, and not do a thing, when we should have been working.

That's what I saw happen with some of the employees who I hired on a whim. They were hourly without set hours since I wanted to provide the freedom of flexibility and ability to work when they could. Yet they would clock hours for talking to each other about non-client things or clock hours without approval in order to help each other's author careers. They would clock hours for working on a project together without letting me know when it was only one person who was supposed to be working on it, and it would still take double the time I expected it to. I had the wrong people in roles where they would do something, then I'd have to pay to have someone else come in and fix it.

They didn't see it was damaging to a small business that needed to be lean and efficient. I didn't see the damage until it was too late. Even then, it would take me months to fire someone when I should have done it the moment I realized it.

Yet I didn't want to upset them or look bad, so I sacrificed the survival of the company to keep someone in a seat who didn't belong.

Unfortunately, I didn't make a move to fix it until it was dire.

The failures were stacking on top of each other, and the only way it would change was by me learning how to be a real CEO. Yes, I didn't expect to become that. Never did I expect to lead an actual company. But now that I was in that position, I had the choice to either forfeit the role and stay where I was comfortable, or fight for what I knew had the potential to become something really good.

Thank God I am fueled by learning because I chose to fight and my character and dreams strengthened as a result. But I had to go through many more hardships and failure first.

bold, not weak

I'VE SPENT THE MAJORITY OF MY LIFE TALKING IN question marks, as though I'm constantly seeking approval.

I was teaching Easton to read when he was six, and he would read a word that he knew, but yet look up at me for confirmation. "The..." (Look up at me.) "Cat..." (Look up at me.) "Sat..." (Look up at me.) "On..." (Look up at me.)

I kept coaching him, "Don't look at me. Look within yourself. Trust yourself. Just sound out the words. You'll be fine." He has done the same thing when playing sports; he's always looking at me while on the field or on the court. I constantly remind him to focus on the team, the ball, the game, not on approval from me.

This kid of mine is brilliantly creative and when he's being himself without influence from anyone else, he is inquisitive, sweet, and passionate about learning. There is so much about him that makes me constantly see *me* as a little girl. I have as much compassion as I do fear that the same things that brought me down may bring him down as well.

The hardest part is seeing my own lack of confidence reflected in him and having no clue how to correct it. I'm always telling him stories about how I would behave as a child, and how much that held me back. I want him to learn from what I went through so he doesn't have the same experiences. I want him to learn from my mistakes. I want him to see that when we're seeking others' approval, we're not operating at 100% because we are casting doubts in every thought we have and action we take. We're performing at less than we're capable of because we're stopping short to seek approval that we're on track instead of giving it all we've got and *knowing* that's enough.

But when I'm also doubting what I'm saying as I'm speaking, how can I expect him to do anything other than mirror exactly what I'm doing?

I often wonder how long exactly I have spoken in question marks. I cringe when I catch myself doing it. I'm half-seeking approval and half-seeking confirmation that I'm being heard. *Am I saying this right? Am I getting this right? Do you like what I'm saying? Are you hearing me at all?*

What I realized is that I was constantly thinking not about what I want or feel, but about how I could flex and adjust based on someone else's reaction. I was constantly reading others and making sure however I responded, it was a fit for what they expected of me. The best thing I did for myself was shut that off, but that only came with age and the exhaustion of trying to read minds and be everything for everyone, instead of just being me.

As I've gotten more confident in my poise and presence over the past couple of years, either from simply aging, experiences, or both, I've come to notice how my voice is still not confident in times that I expect it to be.

In my mind, my words are bold. I am awesome. What I want to say is powerful and inspiring and incredible! But when I try to push those words out of my mouth, the outcome is anything but the vision in my mind. I struggle. My voice and words sound weak. They're not like I imagined. They're not like the voice in my head. And I wish I could mirror what I'm projecting inside. I don't know where the disconnect is from my brain to my mouth.

My mom has that. She often stumbles over what she's saying, attempting to find the right word, veering off into a different direction than she intended when she started the sentence. When I was younger, I used to avoid being around her. I blamed her for my own oratory issue, as though it was contagious. Now that I'm older, I see that my mom was speaking from her heart, which is further from our mouth than our head is, so it kind of does make sense. What I should have been focused on when I was younger was where she was speaking from, because that's what I adopted and I'm proud of it. Nonetheless, just because we may inherit certain tendencies from our parents or environment, it doesn't mean we can't break free of them.

I wasn't completely shocked when both of my boys ended up with speech delays, but I wanted better for them. They were diagnosed with what's called childhood apraxia of speech. It's an actual disconnect between what the brain is trying to communicate to the mouth and jaw muscles and the subsequent sounds and words.

I'm not sure mine is an actual diagnosable condition, or if it's a lack of confidence since an early age at the core. It's almost a chicken or egg sort of question: Is it the way I spoke that created my lack of confidence, or is it my lack of confidence that affected the way I speak? That "Pump Up the Jam" video that makes me cringe, the dodgeballs thrown at me for my accent, the way my ex-husband would leave the room in the middle of my sentence, rejection at school play auditions and speech contest losses, talking to people where they don't hear me at all—despite our proximity.

All I know for sure is that I desperately want to be stronger in my delivery, and it's regularly brought to my attention. There's a lot inside, constantly rolling around in my head, and one of my biggest frustrations is when it doesn't come out as I expect.

Knowing that language is just as much about communication as it is a reflection of our personal identity makes me want to improve my delivery even more. I want to be confident in all forms.

My written words can be weak as well, even though I've typically made efforts to edit them as much as possible. I've noticed a trend, specifically with women, where we cushion our words with phrases such as: "I think," "I feel," or "I believe," as well as words like "just," "maybe," or "possibly" instead of being bold with exactly what is on our mind. We're hedging our language, and usually it's in an attempt to foster harmony and avoid conflict.

Stepping in this CEO role especially has forced me to see the gaps occurring between the strength I feel inside and what I'm projecting. It's made me realize the importance in taking ownership over what's been given to me to protect. It took stepping into that role, and almost losing my business, for me to see how I needed to start operating, not just professionally, but personally as well.

Four words that have been coming up for me this year are: voice, boundaries, integrity, and dominion. I originally saw them as separate feats I had to set out to learn, work on, and improve, until I understood they go hand-in-hand.

My boundaries have been challenged in both my personal and professional life. What I realized in this resurfacing pattern is that I never actually had clear boundaries. As in, never.

Especially while operating in my natural people-pleaser mode, I wanted more than anything to not upset or offend someone. I *needed* to be known as the nice girl. So instead, I flexed and bent over and over to do what's right for others instead of doing what I know is right. I didn't want to have something I wanted (a business opportunity, my reputation, a friendship, peace in the environment, etc.) taken away as a punishment for disappointing someone. Truth is, I was terrified of coming off as "mean," and it's funny writing that out because it doesn't seem like something to be scared of, but people pleasers will understand. Sometimes I'd be terrified to appear unprofessional, even though what I learned is that having boundaries is *more* professional, not less.

In this process of deconstructing my beliefs over the past few years and building, repairing, creating new ones, the one thing I wasn't doing was having clear standards on what I am for and what I'm against; of what I will allow in my life, and what I will not; of how I will be treated and what I will not tolerate. Give me someone I care about, and I will advocate to the death in order to protect their boundaries; yet here I was, operating from a lack of under-standing of my own.

My lack of boundaries enabled employees and clients to bull-doze us, disrespect us, and take advantage of us. Taking note of this in my professional life made me see it directly related to a pattern in my personal life. In my head, the story I told myself was that I was going above and beyond for other people; but the only narrative I was projecting is that I was someone who wasn't strong enough to stand in her own convictions—because they weren't defined.

Which is really interesting because I had identified these things when I was nine years old in the original "One Burning Soul" essay collection. For heaven's sake, my company was based on that with being called Burning Soul Press. God was preparing me for years in advance. But as an adult, it's like I couldn't recall what my bound-aries were because I had crossed the line so many times in the years since, those lines had become stamped out.

The revelation forced me to identify and implement boundaries quicker than I ever had before to prevent the situations that were wrecking me bit by bit.

Part of establishing my boundaries was identifying my values. One, especially, became incredibly important in the past few years since I saw a noticeable effect of the lack of it.

When my ex-husband made the promise that he would support my writing career, and then went back on it, looping in conditions, I lost an extreme amount of trust in him. That trust continued to deteriorate when he repeated this pattern, his words unsupported by actions, which was often. My frustration multiplied when I heard him make promises to the kids without follow-through—and that's when I recognized that I was doing it too.

My ex-husband and I seemed to bond most over our flaws. We could find comfort in each other because our worst traits were being reflected in the other person so we didn't have to be ashamed. Despite words being so important to me all this time, I didn't recog-nize how loosely I used them until I saw the same thing in him. Whether it be telling people I was sick when I didn't want to follow through with an event I had committed to or telling the kids it would be "a couple minutes" before I could come play, yet allowing that to turn into fifteen minutes. Every circumstance felt justifiable, but ultimately, I was lacking in integrity.

Rather than embrace the reflection of a shared flaw, as I had in the past, it was a wake-up call. As a fiercely protective mom, I didn't want my kids to be hurt, to lose trust, or inherit the same patterns. I realized I needed to be in alignment with my values, because I want to be a better representation for my kids.

Integrity of my words has become a high value of mine, even down to saying I'll call someone "in two minutes," and making sure I do. If I commit to attending something, I show up. I don't make excuses if I don't want to go to something; I just say I'm not interested. If I don't follow through with something because I forgot, I truly feel bad about it. I'm still working on this because I'm breaking many years of bad habits, but it has become important enough for me to constantly be aware and intentional.

As I'm operating from a place of integrity and boundaries, I realized I no longer worry about other people's reactions as much as I once did. It has made me bolder and comfortable in truth and the purity of my intentions. It removed a layer of guilt that I had been carrying for most of my life as I realized all my concerns stemmed from misalignment. Integrity was a value that always existed, but until I came into harmony with it, I couldn't see it for what it was.

Dominion, on the other hand, was a word that not only did I not apply in my life, but also one that I hadn't yet considered. Dominion, in essence, is sovereignty. Ownership. Authority over an area. Suddenly, it was showing up everywhere, even in a dream. In the dream, I watched as the roots of a beautiful oak tree sunk deeper and deeper into the ground and the limbs and leaves sprouted everywhere. I was on top of it, watering it, and I heard a voice say, "This is your dominion. The one of sharing our people's stories."

When I had that dream, I immediately recognized how I had fallen short in owning that calling in my business, despite being in the business of capturing people's stories. Sure, I was doing it but I wasn't doing it with the authority that I was called to lead it in. I was still operating in passivity, telling people how they should do something but being way too soft when they wouldn't follow through or follow our protocols because I didn't want to appear like I didn't have compassion for their unique personalities or their situations.

When it comes to dominion over my household and my children, I no longer rely on my expectations of what my ex-spouse should do as their dad. I take an active stance in providing for them, protecting them, guiding them. That means advocating for the kids instead of expecting their dad to do it as the man, or instead of getting frustrated when he's not practicing with them between baseball games, I'm getting out on the field (in spite of my poor skills) and practicing with the boys instead. I'm not playing a role that was given to me; I'm taking ownership of a role that *matters* to me.

Something amazing happens when our boundaries are defined and our dominion is clarified: our voices strengthen. It allows us to have a powerful stance to operate from. We don't slink back and let others steal the areas we've been called to watch over. We rise up and take ownership, protecting those things as much as we'd protect our own kids or anything else important to us.

It has taken me a long time to realize that embracing the fullest expression of myself doesn't harm or offend others, nor does it diminish anyone else. I no longer wish to live a life where I hold back, operating at just 50% of my true potential, constantly trying to conform to perceived expectations or fit in. Embracing more of my authentic self enables me to better fulfill the purpose that God has designed for me. With a clear understanding of who I am and a defined mission, I can confidently be bold, knowing that I am here to make a meaningful impact in this world. Now I'm willing to do what it takes to protect that and see it through.

breathing, not suffocating

When we decided to move to Tennessee, we had to scramble to buy a house. The market was insanely competitive. Everyone was flocking to Tennessee, it seemed, from all over the country during the COVID era. My ex-husband took a lot of trips back and forth to try to find a house, attempting to put an offer in, but everyone was paying over asking, and we lost out on house after house. Eventually we lucked out and got one in what turned out to be the best place we could be.

Two months later, we made the decision to divorce.

We lived under the same roof when we were first separated, not wanting to throw the kids off more by an immediate divorce layered on top of the recent move. Besides, house prices were at an all-time high, so it wasn't easy for one of us to move out.

In the mornings, I usually would stay in bed and wait until he returned to his room upstairs. I became an observer of the life we once lived together, listening to how he spoke to the kids and the dog... and realizing how much of it was based in control. I don't think it was his intention, but it was his default operating mode. I understand that at the core, it's fear-based—I have my own control issues, namely with anything related to the safety of the kids. But it was in those moments, I started to understand more of why I felt the way I did with him.

When I'm in my home space, or anyplace that I feel somewhat safe, I'm a wild and free soul. My thoughts are wild, my dreams are lofty, and anything is possible, which goes against the controlled environment and life he wants to have. When I violated his or traditional expectations, he struggled. When he couldn't see possibilities in life and the world the way I see them, I struggled. Things grew tense. Fights ensued. He wanted structure and a tight grip on everything; I didn't. I felt like there was nothing I could do that was right, and I'm sure he felt the same.

It was stifling for me as an independent creative to live in a place that's filled with so much control and order. It doesn't make his preferred way of life wrong; but how we like our environments to be created massive conflict.

I would feel like I had to be proactive at all times and launch into control-mode too because I couldn't stand the air when he became mad or frustrated. It's like operating as a child again and not wanting to displease my dad, so I started changing who I was and what I needed to do in order to avoid negativity. I was losing myself as a result and becoming way more controlling than I wanted to be as a mom.

I grew so tired of the frustrated remarks and visible disappointment. I got so tired of everything feeling like a compromise between us, because we both lost, instead of working together like a married couple should. Unhappiness was constantly clogging the air.

I kept telling myself I didn't have a reason to complain and feel so caged when other women have it much worse. He was a nice guy. He was a good dad. He did things around the house like cooked and cleaned when I know many guys aren't known for that. And of course, his money—as though a financial provider by itself is enough. When things weren't going well, he bought me things, and I leaned into it because it reminded me of my dad bringing me animal crackers when he'd be gone for extended times. A gift to fill the void. So, I tried to be happy with "good enough," even if every day made me feel less of a person. Even if I was suffocating.

I just wanted freaking wild freedom.

When I first moved out, I was relieved to have my own space and not have to worry about the tension. Initially, I felt strangely wonderful, like I was breathing for the first time in a long time. I felt like I was finally getting my wild creativity back, and suddenly had more motivation than what I had been able to find in a long time.

Yet despite the shift, one morning in 2023, a little over a year after I had moved out, I had the epiphany that I don't breathe—not in the way I *should* be breathing. And if we don't breathe properly, that's how various forms of suffocation occur, something I felt frequently, whether blaming it on my lack of pursuing my dreams, COVID, or the marriage I had just left.

So, I started taking deeper breaths. I was walking the dogs during the early morning hours, listening to my Spotify playlist, "Remembering Truth," which is a collection of some of my favorite Christian songs. And I started breathing in and out deeply as we walked. I reminded myself that every step is done with God, and I can let go because I'm His.

And for a moment, it worked. I remembered what it was like to breathe fully and deeply. For a moment, I tricked myself into believing that perhaps I broke the barrier that I held within. It was only temporary, though. Without conscious thought, I went right back to breathing with tightness in my chest. Apparently, that had become my standard operating mode, and I didn't like it.

If breathing is supposed to be instinctive, then why is it taking so much conscious thought for me to do it fully?

With the recognition of not breathing fully, I could feel the aches in my back, the physical toll it was taking on me. Systematically, I know if I'm not breathing deeply, it's affecting my health elsewhere. Perhaps that's why I have several clients who advocate and educate on the importance of breathing. I just wasn't listening to the signs that the message was for me.

I seem to breathe the best when I'm alone, and I don't want that to be the only time I'm able to.

I think my breath is shallow because somewhere at sometime, I lost faith in what was good and true, and lived in anticipation of the bad. I blocked happenstances and blessings that were meant to occur by avoiding anything that could go wrong.

I was in a book club with an amazing group of women, and one of the questions posed was, "If someone from a dealership drove up with your dream car, the perfect style, the perfect color, maxed out with all the bells and whistles you want, and handed you the keys and said, 'It's yours,' what would you do?" Everyone mostly answered, "I would hop right in, thank God, and drive off!"

My honest answer, even though it's not the one I wish I would have, was, "I'd hop in and take it, and then check the mail every day, waiting for the bill to come in."

That honest reflection hit me hard. Here I was, wondering why God wasn't bringing obvious miracles in my life in moments I needed them since times had gotten tough. But why would He bring miracles if I'd still doubt that they were indeed from Him? If I'd be waiting for the shoe to drop, the rug to be pulled out from under my feet, and any other idiom you can come up with that would showcase the most obvious fact: I don't trust when good things happen, so I hold my breath, waiting for the bad, instead of breathing, relaxing, and trusting the good.

I absolutely exhaust myself with this automatic, self-protection mechanism that's operating almost 24/7. For every situation that arises in my life, my brain is already preparing an emergency disaster plan for the 100 ways each can go wrong and what I'm going to do to save myself from hurt, disappointment, or worse. When I'm not breathing completely, it's because I'm lacking the trust. I'm clenching, nervous, scared, anxious.

How did I get to this place?

My gut-reaction answer to this question would have been to provide a list of all the times I've been burned, hurt, let down, disappointed, taken advantage of, and violated. I may have referred to all the times I thought prayers were left unanswered, that I cried out and was seemingly ignored, that I believed my control of the situation is what protected me in the end.

In essence, I'd give all my justifications to why I should be less trusting and not more trusting. *Look at the proof in my life.*

But I know the real truth: My fear blocked all the times things could have been so much better, and my control as a result blocked all the times that things could have been so much easier.

When I was making the eight-hour trek from my house to the college I attended my freshman year, Northwestern College in Iowa, I would drive with the heat on and the windows down when it was cold outside. I loved the combination of the heat with the frigid air. I know I was breathing deeply then. During that drive, I felt so incredibly in tune with God, free, rooted in Him, and full of faith that He had me no matter what, that I felt as though I could let go of the wheel, close my eyes, and still arrive safely no matter what.

One of my favorite things is that every time I'm either picking Camden up from school or his dad drops him off, he comes flying at me. Running as fast as he can, max speed, he jumps into my arms. Usually, he leaps further than he should to be safely caught. Every time, he trusts I'm going to catch him, so he gives it his all, and I catch him every time. That trust in someone represents freedom, and that's what I've found as I grow closer in my relationship with God. I've had to let go of all the details and circumstances that have defined my trust in the past, and leap into God's arms, knowing I'll always be caught.

We were made to breathe, and to breathe deeply, just like the plants and living things in nature were designed to do as well. In the end, it doesn't matter why I'm not breathing fully, but I need to get back to doing it. Breath brings life, and there's a lot of life I plan on living yet.

free, not trapped

AT MY SECOND WEDDING, ONE OF MY BRIDESMAIDS TOLD me, "You look awkward dancing. You just need to let go." She wasn't wrong. I've been told multiple times by others, "Just let loose. *Feel* it."

In my head and when I'm by myself, I'm so damn free. But when I try to live that way from the inside out, I go stiff, especially when eyes are on me.

My body feels like a barrier between the outwardly perceived me and the wild soul on the inside. I don't know how to get them to work in tandem.

I felt awkward dancing because I didn't know how to *be* in my own skin, especially with other people around. Instead, I was obsessed with what other people thought of me, something I later realized was heavily entwined with my people-pleasing tendencies, as though every element of me had to please someone else or there was no purpose in my existence. So if I didn't dance well and it wasn't purposeful to someone else, I was failing and it was another reason for me to shrink.

There was a time that I did dance, or at least tried to. When I moved to Grand Rapids, Michigan after college, I would venture out to a popular club there called The B.O.B. I went with a small group of girlfriends the first time. We were in the middle of the dance floor, I was trying to move my hips and body the way they were, sweat dripping from the mental effort more than the physical exertion. I finally felt I was getting in the groove. A few guys started dancing with us—except *us* turned into *them* because I was the only one standing on the outside of the group. I got pushed out. I could only assume it's because I was such an awkward dancer. So now every time I try to dance, that's in the back of my mind, fueling the negative self perception that I really cannot dance—at all. I tend to avoid public dancing situations whenever I can.

Recently, an opportunity presented itself when I was at a concert with a friend. I wanted to dance, I was feeling the music, and I'm older now, so I'm more comfortable in my skin—but I still didn't know what to do with my hands. Yes, that excuse came back, but it's true. I felt so weird. I couldn't move the way I wanted to move. I was stiff, and soon gave up.

Once I had my kids, I started dancing with them, which is always a blast. We all laugh and are totally breathless by the end. I can only seem to dance when they're around and no one else. Even they seem embarrassed of me at times, but I give it my all anyhow.

It was in those dance parties with my kids, where I was safe and happy, that I began noticing something vital. I realized I had never actually used every muscle before. I had never allowed my soul to fill out my entire body. I'd never really connected my soul *with* my body. So when it comes to things like dancing, I'd never fully been present in my body enough to be able to move every part. I didn't know how to get all the pieces to flow because I was so disconnected.

It was like I was scared of feeling trapped inside, when instead my body was allowing me to be free—if I could just trust that it was safe.

This epiphany was eye-opening. I realized I hadn't been using the gift of my body in the way I should have been for most of my life and it was creating a disconnect that had become my way of living.

Writing my memoir throughout the year before this moment

helped me understand this more because it gave me a bird's-eye view of the patterns of my life.

Giving my body away is a theme that showed up. Like with the way I've given my body over to men who weren't careful or caring time and again. So it kept me disconnected from my body instead of attached to it. I didn't value it.

And it's not just reserved to my body, it's like I'm constantly weighing what parts of me I can give away in order to get something from someone else. Like I'm some sort of chained, sacrificial entity, reserved for whoever wants to take a piece. At the core, was the need to be liked, to be loved, to be cared for, to be accepted. And rarely did any of those feelings actually fulfill me long-term. Also, the majority of the times I did that, those people I exchanged parts of myself to please, whether strangers, friends, relationships, or clients, are no longer in my life.

In all the times in my life I gave up pieces of myself, decreased my worth, or allowed myself to be damaged for someone else's temporary wants, desires, or needs, I could have stepped back. I could have thought, *Is it worth it? Is this truly an equal exchange?* If my perspective was rooted in love for myself instead of a desperation to be loved, I would have said, "No. Absolutely not."

Sometimes I wonder if that's part of what I was meant to learn in the past few years. It started with my children. I realized how desperately I wanted them to see their worth and know they never, ever have to exchange it for the approval of others. Especially trying to please somebody who doesn't honor them, or truly care about them, and will only be in their life for such a small blip, they'll have trouble remembering their name. And yet, when that wasn't enough for me to turn the mirror toward myself and be stronger in my own worth, the struggle came. I broke. I had to face all my demons, all my wrong decisions, all at once.

I've realized how much I've seen my body as a separate piece of me, when in fact, we are the whole self. We are indivisible entities and though it's easy to talk about our minds, hearts, souls, and bodies as separate—they are attached. They all work together, and sometimes I feel like part of my quest here in life is to get them in sync. No debate between what my mind is telling me vs. what my heart feels. Not my mind shutting down because my body is experiencing something my brain can't even bring itself to record in memory.

I've had three very realistic dreams in my life. So real that I had trouble waking because it felt like I was already awake. In each one, I met angels or Jesus. In two of the three, I died by a tornado to get there, apparently a homage to the tornado alley I grew up in.

The first one I had was when I had yet to have kids and was in my first marriage. The clouds in the sky moved rapidly above a table I sat at with a group of other people as an angel appeared in the sky. The angel approached me, and I was able to ask him questions. A lot of them were about my life decisions at that time, one being I knew I wanted to get divorced but I really wanted kids. Suddenly I could see the past, present, and future all entwined. I could see the kids at different ages. I could see myself. The angel said the choice has always been mine to make.

In another dream, a year after the first one took place, after I died, I went to heaven and was being given a tour by Jesus. I was shown where I would live and the room had this huge, horizontal window where I could change the scenery to anything I wanted. There were the most magnificent and realistic scenes outside the window, nature in motion. I was told the choice was mine to make.

What I took from both of those dreams is that our choices are *ours*, and we were never meant to feel trapped in previous choices we made. But understanding what true freedom is, is important as well.

I had to redefine what my definition of freedom really is. Previously, I thought I needed the acceptance of someone else before I could get into such a place. I thought freedom was found in being loved by someone else enough to be myself, so I put expectations on others to create an environment for me that I could be myself. That was unfair to important people in my life. I should have focused on what I could control all along, which was my reaction to the circumstances. I should have stayed focused on creating the environment that I wanted, knowing I could influence it just as much as I was letting the opposite influence take control, but it meant being secure in who I was to be able to do that.

I can now say that I'm secure in who I am and I no longer feel trapped by the past. I am complete. I am whole. I am forgiven.

Now that I understand my true worth, my soul knows it fully belongs in my body because I'm safe; I'm in God's hands. And I've learned that when I stand in the truth that I'm loved unconditionally by God, I can feel free in *any* situation.

unified, not separated

DESPITE MY GENERAL DISINTEREST IN WEDDINGS, I always cried during the father-daughter dance. I loved those moments. I had a strange fear that I wouldn't be able to have that dance with my dad, which is why I rushed into marriage number one, oddly enough. It's like I somehow thought that magical moment would make up for all the other moments we lost and I wanted my shot at it before he passed away.

I harbored a lot of hurt from my dad for many years, but in more recent years, I've started seeing my dad differently.

Several years ago, my parents were visiting our house in Bloomington when suddenly, Dad went down with excruciating pain. Outside of a migraine, I've never seen my dad admit he was in pain, especially not to the point where he cries out. Now, he was crying for help because of how badly it hurt.

I was scared it was his heart. We called 911. An ambulance came, pulled out the stretcher, and worked to get him secured so they could get him down from the second floor, out the door, and to the hospital.

I was terrified to hear the sounds my dad made. I didn't know what was happening and feared it may have been the end.

As they were trying to get my dad into the ambulance, a slew of neighbors I didn't even know lined up outside, gawking. No one offered to help. No one did anything, they just stood there and stared.

I was pissed. It was the first time I remember getting defensive about my dad. I glared at each one of them, then I asked them to stop staring—it was none of their business. I didn't want my dad to be wheeled out, in extreme pain, while people he didn't know stared. I wanted to protect him and felt like it was my job to do so. The tables had turned.

At the hospital, they determined a kidney stone was what knocked the big man down. He had to go through a few procedures to get the stone out. Coupled with his heart procedures, since heart disease runs in our family, it was a lot in a short amount of time. I worried about him and prayed over him daily for a year.

Seeing that weakness in Dad made me start seeing him as I should have all along. My dad was just a man dealing with his own history and emotions. I'm not sure if he knows it, but his mortality brought me to the first step of forgiveness and bridging the gap between us. Around that time, I also stopped sobbing over father-daughter dances. I was on the path to healing.

I had wanted to move out of Illinois for a few years, but after my dad's medical emergencies, I felt more inclined to stay there. However, once my ex-husband's brother and sister-in-law decided they were going to move to Tennessee, my ex-husband finally decided he would move, too. In a time when it felt like I could finally grow closer to my dad, we were moving further away.

So, although I was frustrated that it took someone else to convince my ex-husband to move, I was also ready for a change of scenery. I'd wanted to live in Tennessee since I was ten years old, after having memories of the best family vacations to Gatlinburg when I was a little girl. We looked at several places, but decided on the south Nashville area, ironically the same exact town as his brother and sister-in-law.

At this time, a new trigger for my random sobs surfaced. Anytime I saw an example of a man being there for his wife, or a man fighting to keep his woman, whether on TV or in a real life scenario, it would be enough to start the waterworks. A new pain became clear. I wanted to be fought for in my relationship, and wasn't feeling it at all.

When we were separated, I reached out to him a few times to ask how he was feeling about everything. I asked him if it was worth having a discussion—to see if there was still something between us. He would avoid the question.

I even did this a week before our court date. I asked if he thought it was worth getting lunch together to talk.

He replied, "I can't even talk about that."

That's the thing, we could never talk about it. We could never talk about *anything*.

One of the most common thoughts I had throughout our relationship and even afterward was, *If only you would talk to me, that's all it would take to save this...*

I was tired of fighting for a real connection with the person I was once supposed to spend life with. I knew that once the kids were out of the house, we wouldn't have anything to talk about, because we already didn't have anything to talk about. It didn't seem worth it to wait for that moment to declare the end of the marriage.

The moment we agreed to divorce, I told him it could go one of two ways. We could have it be horrible and tense and ugly, like everyone expects divorces to be, or we could be mature and make sure that nothing but love remained, in order to raise the kids right.

I had to fight to keep that unity in the first year, choosing love over and over again above all else. Because no matter our circumstances, I wanted to be a family unit. The kids deserved it even if it looked different than what was expected and preferred. It was possible, and I was determined to make it be. There have been times post-divorce that I have told him I love him. For no reason beyond that he is the father of our boys. Those boys will always keep us unified and I will forever treat him like family.

If I had my way to this day, I'd still want my kids to spend their nights in only one household we all share. I almost want to say, "I would do anything to make it easier for them," but I'm not sure having two parents who never truly talk to each other is what's best either. I want them to have a healthy example of a marriage, and we weren't it.

I debated changing my name legally back to my maiden name for fear of further separation, but I had already been using my maiden name for my business and books for years, so it just made sense. I'm still called by their last name at doctor's offices and the school, and I know that'll just be a part of the rest of my life.

Three months after the divorce was finalized, he shared that he'd been in a serious relationship for about nine months. I met his girlfriend at the coffee shop so we could talk before she met the boys. I shared with her my vision of unity no matter our circumstances and that we'd come together to support the boys no matter what. She had the same vision, and it was wonderful knowing we could be successful in this co-parenting relationship that now involved significant others.

I am really proud of our co-parenting relationship, though I know it takes a lot of effort to maintain both of our parts. We are intentional about doing things as a family unit, including spending time at each other's houses. We seem to talk more as co-parents than we did as spouses, and I'm optimistic that we can maintain this for the years to come, since I believe we've gotten past the worst of it.

I recently had a friend, who was going through a separation, stay with me for a few days. They had been separated, but still lived under the same roof until it reached a breaking point and he needed to move out. I offered my guest bedroom since we're neighbors, until he could find some other place, or, ideally, move back home.

Every night he was here, we talked about how their marriage ended up where it was. I talked about my marriage and shared my perspective. He was hurting badly from being away from his two young girls and felt like he was letting them down. I understood that feeling all too well.

What I told him about my marriage one night shocked even me.

"I needed to get away from him because I needed a chance to become who I was meant to be, and I wasn't able to do that while with him. However, if I could have had the chance to become who I am today while still living under the same roof to be there for my kids, I would choose that in a heartbeat. If he asked me to move back in, I would. Because getting my kids 50% of the time is not enough."

My confession helped my friend realize that being alone and starting over and getting the kids only 50% was not worth it. He went back to his wife to give it another try. I was grateful that my experience could help someone else, and show them what's on the other side.

I didn't go into the deeper details, though... about how dating is just about as bad as every lonely night I had in my marriage. The nights I cry just wanting my kids here and hating that I'm missing so many special moments. How empty this house feels when they're not here and that it took almost two years before I finally adjusted to the silence and the loneliness of it all.

I didn't tell him about the bitterness I really have to fight against, knowing my ex got the things I should have, like the house, the stability of not having to move multiple times like I was forced to do. He got a new girlfriend right away, while here I am, single as can be, and sometimes it's hard to be happy for him, instead of unhappy with what I don't have and want.

Though it sucked to have all of this happen right when we moved to Tennessee, ironically the best part is that it happened here.

My ex found what seems to be his future wife (the first time I met her over coffee, she told me that he was "her person," which was actually neat to hear) and I found a new family. Things we wouldn't have found if we divorced before moving here because we never would have ended up here otherwise.

Moving to Tennessee meant discovering what real community is for the first time in my life. It started the moment we first arrived in the driveway with a car full of stuff after a seven-hour drive. We met ten of our neighbors instantly as they flooded around us. We met more people in our Tennessee neighborhood within ten minutes of being here than we knew in nearly all our time living in our Illinois neighborhood.

It was hard to move out of that house after the divorce because those neighbors became friends and I loved how close everyone on the street was, which was a fun new concept. I'm glad my kids get to grow up with their kids still, but I hate missing out on living there, too.

After I moved out, I started going to a coffee shop that I quickly fell in love with. That coffee shop became a lifeline for me when I felt like I was losing everything else. The atmosphere was noticeably different. It made me feel like I could be myself without pretense and be comfortable, at ease, and I felt inspired to write again in brand-new ways.

At first, I couldn't explain why it felt different at this coffee shop; it just did every second I was there. One day, I overheard someone saying that the beautiful barn that also sat on the property turned into a church on Sundays, and that the church actually owned the coffeehouse and the entire forty-acre property. As soon as I heard this, I went to the church service the next day, which happened to be a Sunday, and brought my boys with me.

Walking into the barn for the first time, I knew I was home, just like that coffeeshop had already become. There was no stage. The congregation sat in a circle around the band and pastor on a leveled floor so they could see each other during the service instead of staring straight ahead. People were welcoming, but not in a fake way; in a genuine, "I want to get to know you" sort of way. People worshiped with their hands in the air, with all their might, even men. Those men looked like my dad but they weren't reserved like the men I was used to; they were free. They showed pure emotion.

I knew I wanted my boys to see men embrace their vulnerability and faith in the same way and be part of a church like that. I attended every Sunday since, and the more I got to know people, the more they felt like family. True family. I knew that if something happened in my life, I could reach out to them and they'd be there for me. I didn't have to hide in shame that I am a twice-divorcee or any of my other past stories that would normally keep me with my head down in a church. There was no "you have to be somebody perfect to be accepted here" energy.

I felt like I wanted to give everything I could by donating my time to help it operate, to function, to be there for the people. That's when the concept of a real community sunk in.

I also realized that's why the atmosphere at the coffee shop was so different. The church family was in and out of those doors constantly, people regularly meeting, hugging, praying for each other. It's like a continual family reunion, not just excited to see each other on Sundays, but all days of the week. It's crazy that in all the time I was at the coffee shop, I missed that; but now that I know the people, I see how it was all around me the entire time.

Within weeks of attending, my relationship with Christ had deepened. I was being challenged in beautiful ways not to just live out my relationship with God on Sunday, but every single day of the week and every single minute of my days.

I realized that, unfortunately, I didn't value family or community in my life until I started going to this church. They became instantly important to me. They were my example of true love and redemption and family, even when completely different people come together. I had felt alone for so long that at first it felt uncomfortable to want to be a part, to immediately care about people I barely knew, and feel so vulnerable. But it was exactly what I was missing in my life.

This church community, as well as the people who I've met at the coffeehouse outside of the church, have become my extended family. I've never felt so protective of a group of people, even with some that I have yet to know. I feel loyal to them because being my true self is enough to be a part of it. I don't have to pretend to be anyone else. I don't have to manipulate situations. I don't have to worry that I'm breaking any rules or high expectations of how to act. I can just show up, be me, and love freely.

Once I recognized how much being there was shaping my

values, I understood my part in the gaps that existed in my own family unit. My brothers and I all call ourselves the black sheep of the family, which should say quite a bit. We feel like individually, we are the odd ones out, and that feeling created a divide instead of us still loving each other thoroughly and coming together.

Being a part of the church family raised the importance for me to prioritize the people who have been there my entire life, as much as I was valuing and prioritizing this new community. I started calling my parents and brothers more, telling them I love them, asking them how they were. Little things that people in other families may do, but mine was not close-knit in that way. I realized that could change with some tweaks, and I wanted to do just that.

As independent as I can be, I don't want to do things alone anymore. I want family and community in a way I've never wanted them before. Whether it's in forming this new look of what our immediate family is going to look like with co-parenting and spouses, or finding new smaller communities, I want my kids to know that they are fully supported and part of a bigger system that loves them for who they are. Even if our family members are further away, we can still have adopted families closer in proximity.

My kids are going to grow up in an expanded and closer family than what I had growing up, in which not all members are blood, and that's really freaking cool. They'll have instilled in them the importance of having a strong community around us, and the value of protecting it as much as participating in it, understanding who they are and what they do *matter* in the world around them.

To some, the move to Tennessee may have looked like it separated our family, but what it did was multiply and enrich our family. It's turned into one of the greatest moves we could have made and one of the greatest gifts we've ever had.

hungry, not starving

Since the divorce, I've started dating again. And it's been... interesting.

One of the biggest signs I was ready for divorce was when other men started crossing my mind more than my husband. I blamed it on about a billion things, but if I could have pegged the word at the time, "unfulfilled" would have been the word. Unfulfilled, not just from the relationship, but because I didn't know what it meant to be fulfilled *before* I entered a relationship with him. Of course, like every other relationship in my life, I expected him to fulfill me.

My ex-husband and I had a gap growing between us before I started my business, but starting my business and diving even deeper into the personal development field made it a chasm that spread as wide as it did deep—and fast. I was involved in incredible programs alongside men who were excited about growth, not professionally, but internally and emotionally. My ex didn't share a growth-oriented mindset. So while I was changed and evolved into what I felt like was the best version of myself, he stayed the same. I'd be excited about things that he wasn't. It's not like we ever had too many deep conversations, but after a while, conversation dwindled over time until they only involved day-to-day exchanges of information or the weather.

In the meantime, I was in awe of these men who were emotionally open, vulnerable, doing big things, and growing in front of my eyes. It created a desire in me, wishing my husband could be like that, and since it was clear he didn't have any desire to be, the longing for a man who was like that grew.

About three months before we made the decision to divorce, I was in an entrepreneurial year-long program. The man leading it was someone I had grown to deeply respect and admire. The first time we met in person for one of the events, there was an undeniable attraction. Our eyes met each other often enough through the event, at a level that went above normal. Of course, I doubted it, because I knew my patterns of being somewhat delusional that a man was feeling what I was feeling. Yet after a full day at this intimate event, it was clear there was more between us. Each time we'd talk, it was amazing, deep, brilliant, energetic. You could almost see the waves pulsating between us in the air. We both fed off it.

After the end of the first day, we had a group dinner at night under the stars. We sat down next to each other and what started out as a group conversation, turned into a one-on-one between him and me. Just like the scenes in movies where the world faded away— that's truly what it was like. Despite the noise around us, it was just us. It felt like the stars had dropped around us and magic was happening. Two days later, he showed me a text from one of his friends (who was a speaker at the event and at the dinner), asking him what was happening that night because there was a clear energetic shift that everyone could feel. Like two people who should be something to each other finally connected.

My ex-husband had come with me on this trip, and when I returned to the Airbnb that night, we went out to dinner. I was so excited about everything I had learned that day. When I tried to tell him about my day and share it with him, it was clear he didn't get it. There was no excitement. No "Oh, I completely understand!" or "That's fascinating!" So we sat in silence for 95% of the meal, despite being away from each other all day. My mind drifted back to the event leader, wondering if he would walk in that restaurant like fate pushing us together. I was anxious to see him again. I had a hunger for conversation, and now I had found it in another guy who satiated my craving.

The morning of day two, the leader and I immediately found each other and we started talking again. It was obvious we were both counting down to seeing each other. Every break, we gravitated toward each other. At the end, we stood outside the venue for a long time, our conversation deepening with each second. We shared everything. The conversation moved into the area of our marriages, and how we both felt unhappy. His wife and he were discussing an open marriage, to avoid separating the family unit and affecting the kids. He said that they recognized that they were not fulfilling each other's wishes for emotional and physical intimacy and wanted to find other people who could.

It was the first time I had heard of the concept of an open marriage being truly lived out—and not by celebrities. It was intriguing because I was unhappy in my marriage, and it seemed to present a viable option to get my husband and me through the next several years with the kids.

The leader drove me back to my Airbnb. Being in the car with him, we both could feel the pull even more, the heat. We talked as though we were already in a relationship, our mutual affection bridging time and space. We didn't do anything, but the temptation was there. We didn't want to say goodbye. We talked about driving off together and just leaving everything behind. I reluctantly left the car and went back to another night with my husband where the TV filled the void that our voices didn't. The event leader and I kept talking via text and voice messages throughout the night, even with our spouses in the next rooms... and that continued night after night.

By the time I got back to normal life, I became curious about this open marriage idea and started researching it. I knew I was already looking at an impending divorce and this was the extra fuel. Now there was a man, who wasn't my spouse, who I couldn't stop thinking about. The connection between us felt unlike anything I

had experienced before, like a true "previous life, spiritual connection" type of depth.

One day, the leader called to tell me he told his wife about me,
and that he wanted me to be his partner in the "open" part of their
marriage. She had already identified hers, too. So they were ready
to move forward. I just needed to figure things out with my
husband.

Until they weren't ready any longer... which didn't take long for
them to figure out. Jealousy reared its ugly head for both of them.
After weeks of counseling, they decided it wasn't smart, and so of
course he found it best to end our relationship and our friendship.
That feeling absolutely sucked. I was really worried I wasn't going to
bounce back. I wrapped a lot of silly thoughts into what could have
been during that time, as though getting half of someone was good
enough.

This made the next four months in his program awkward and
uncomfortable, especially at the last event when his wife made an
obvious presence. She knew who I was—the one her husband
almost chose for their open marriage. By that time, my divorce had
been declared and it hurt that we were in completely two different
places after temporarily feeling like one.

I'm not at all proud of the emotional cheating that took place
and this is another situation that's difficult to write about and
permanently document. However, admittedly in some ways, I'm
glad the situation presented itself. It forced me to acknowledge the
truth in my relationship: we didn't have an emotional, spiritual, or
physical connection. In truth, we barely had it at the beginning of
our relationship, but I didn't find these things important at the
time. My eyes were on building a family and that was all. Naivety
and immaturity at best but it feels embarrassing to admit these
things now.

What I walked away realizing was how much I was starving to
have a partner to talk to and truly connect with, and I no longer
wanted to waste life without one.

When I first thought about dating again, I was excited. Nervous yes, but excited. I was so *starved* for what I had been missing for years.

I hadn't yet broken out of my old ways and patterns though, and that was dangerous.

I was naive. I had rose-colored glasses on. I had tunnel vision. I had all of the above multiplied by ten. I didn't know about terms like "narcissist" or "gas lighting" until I joined a group for women in the area who shared warnings of men they had dated and had a quick lesson in it all.

Then I could see it—but only in hindsight, once I had experienced it myself in this new post-divorce dating world.

The first guy had a "you owe me" mentality and an ego bigger than Nashville itself. He was nice enough, so I got wrapped up in it. I later learned he was a womanizer, who always had at least ten on the hook, and he basically thought that by taking me out on a date and paying, he deserved physical affection. I fell into it because I didn't know boundaries. At all. Besides, it was a thrill to be physical with someone again.

The second guy was addicted to sex, but I didn't see it right away. He was a Midwestern transplant living in Tennessee like me, so we shared many values and bonded over our Midwestern roots. He was the first guy I slept with in this new dating life, and as fun as it was—especially the first night since it had been a *long* time since I had been intimate with someone in that way, I always felt empty afterward.

I was with the third guy the longest. We went "all in" on a relationship, but it was short-lived. It felt like a year, but lasted only a few months. He reminded me of the emo boys I used to have a crush on back in the day. He was an artist, so I loved that, and he taught art. Although, the truth is, I couldn't really get into his art, and that should have been a warning sign. Art is reflective of who we are, and if I felt a void connecting with his art, I should have known it would have been a void with his true colors as well.

He expanded my understanding of what intimacy can be. We'd spend *hours* in bed, naked, as close to each other as possible, not just for sexual activity but while having deep, incredible conversations. Physical, sexual, mental, emotional, spiritual intimacy—everything wrapped together, which made me realize how much I craved exactly that without knowing it. *That's* what I had been missing out on in my marriages.

Just weeks before I met him, I was at home visiting my family. My grandma mentioned how much she missed having nightly conversations with my grandpa who had passed away two years earlier, and I started sobbing out of the blue... I didn't realize until then just how badly I wanted to know what it was like to look forward to talking to someone and talking nonstop every night, like they would do. It gutted me because it was such a deep desire and an emptiness I had put up with for far too long.

And suddenly, I had it in this new relationship... our highs were high but our lows were low. My worth was so low that I let him run over me with lies and manipulation. It took me several months before I realized it, but it hit me after one particularly bad fight. Then, it was like a highlight (or rather, *low*light) reel showing every single time he tried to gaslight me or manipulate me, and placing blame on me for his blow-ups. He was good at being a narcissist and I was good at believing the best in people and only allowing myself to see what I wanted to fill the hole inside. That's a dangerous combination.

That one should have been my warning sign to go into the dating scene with a larger shield. Yet here I was, still believing the best in the men I met and reducing myself to accommodate them because I didn't know how to do it any other way.

Another man I met at a bar. He was wrapped up in his ex-wife and the drama she brought to his life (involving a murder that she was a potential accomplice in, even—yeah, I'll save that for another time). There was a part of me that was convinced that if I had met him before his ex-wife, he wouldn't have been so messed up. So, of course I let it go on for months longer than it should have, listening to him talk about her for hours and hours, as though I expected something to change.

Then I met a man who was everything in so many ways that my heart and soul craved and smelled just like Aaron... but he didn't want me. At first, I thought, *Here we go again. Another Christian man who doesn't think I'm good enough because I'm the dirty, now super sinful twice-divorced seductress.* But clearly he wasn't for me because he held on to my past more than who I was in the present.

Then, I dated another man who was a cop, and also manipulative. He kept saying he wasn't "hungry," which is why despite texting (and sexting) me often, he wasn't asking me out on many dates. I didn't want to push, but toward the end, I realized that was a cop-out (haha, get it?) for truly not giving a damn. I wanted a guy who wanted me. I had spent ten years feeling unwanted as is. This is where I also learned the term *"hungry,"* which I had no usage outside of food prior to this experience. It was also the start of reclaiming my boundaries.

I share these stories not to forever remember these men, but to showcase the wide variety of experiences in a short amount of time. The dating world has not been kind, but it's helped me realize the importance of having boundaries. Something I should have had years ago, but didn't, because, using a spinoff of the cop's phrase, I was *starving.*

What's become clear to me lately, is the difference between starving and being hungry. Hungry is wanting something badly, but realizing we have choices of what we can "eat." Starving is taking anything we can get.

For most of my life, I was starving. Starving to fill a void that I didn't recognize for most of my life. I took scraps because I thought that was all I was worth, all I could get. I did it even as recently as entering the dating world again.

But then I realized I was sick of the belly aches and losing hours of time I couldn't get back from guys who were nothing but a sign in the direction I shouldn't go. I was sick of all my old patterns showing up again even though I should have matured out of them by now.

These experiences provided the exact wake-up call that I needed to change. The revelations worked together with everything else that God was doing in my life at the same time with bringing in people, community, and friendships, while restoring who I was made to be. Now that void I was trying to fill with men doesn't exist because I'm whole whether or not I have a person to share life with.

I'm in a place these days where I'm not seeking out someone, I'm trusting God will bring the right one to me. I don't open myself up to be feasted on by any random man; I'm more protective of what I'm deserving of and I'm saving myself as though it's the first time, repenting and believing I've been restored and redeemed.

Hungry is being mindful of what quenches me on a soul-level and not sacrificing that for temporary fulfillment. I realize the importance of being choosy, of honoring my worth, and knowing the best meal is worth the wait of the preparation.

intimate, not seductive

THERE WAS A KID IN SECOND GRADE WHO REGULARLY smelled like urine because he would pee himself a couple of times weekly in school. Of course at that age, there was no understanding or empathy of it like I have today as an adult and parent, so the way he was made fun of stands out the most. I think that's when I first associated shame with smell. I don't remember many details from childhood, but to this day, I remember his name.

I was recently sharing this memory with a friend who went to a different school and she said, "I remember the kid in second grade who peed all the time, too! I remember his name as well." She went to a different school in a different town, yet it seems maybe everyone knew someone in elementary who peed—and I find it interesting that we don't forget their names.

I may have been a lot of things as a child, but I definitely never wanted to be the smelly kid.

Yet somehow over the past few years, I have developed a fear of becoming the smelly woman.

Whether breath, pits, skin picking up on the odors of the environment, or other sensitive parts, I'm *terrified* of smelling bad. It sucks because I'm literally constantly thinking, *Does my breath smell bad? Do I smell bad? Can people smell me and I can't tell? Have I gotten used to my smell?* I may have had a trace of the fear for a while, but it intensified during the postpartum depression era.

I have gone to multiple doctors to get advice. It is surprisingly awkward to say those words out loud: "I think I smell bad. I need help." Even *they* get uncomfortable. The most frustrating part is that no one seems to ever have any sort of solution. The dermatologist once prescribed me some sort of pill medication but that made my heart feel like it was beating out of my chest. With a family history of heart disease, it wasn't worth it. I'd have to deal with me being stinky over risking my heart shutting down.

I've tried switching to natural remedies. I've tried looking up all the things that could cause it. I don't yet have a solution. I also don't know if I smell this bad, if I'm extra paranoid, or if there are certain parts of me that smell bad, but not all the parts. No one has ever actually told me (yet), it's just something that I'm constantly scared about.

Regardless, feeling like I stink everywhere keeps me from getting close to people, and it's the worst timing because for the first time in my life, I *want* to be around people. The tension I carry for this keeps me a few steps back when all I want to do is bridge the gap. I know I'm being called more than ever to be *with* people to hear their stories, not only on virtual Zoom calls like I have been doing for the past four years. I don't want to *just* have intimate conversations; I want to have them in person, sitting side by side or across a table, and feeling each other's energy as we share.

I have a newfound definition of intimacy and it's important to me because I am finally confident in who I am. I *want* to share myself with others in a healthy way and be there for them.

The thing is, intimacy has always been a tricky concept for me. I've craved it for as long as I can remember, but I have been terrible at receiving it. It's like there's always a reason to keep true intimacy beyond my reach, whether some sort of crazy stench fear, or because I didn't feel I was enough or could be accepted, or because I was scared of what it may turn into.

Intimacy used to be a word that made me feel uncomfortable

because of how I positioned that word to show up through sexual relations only. I always expected a negative situation to occur as a result of opening a door or getting close to someone. Mostly it was because I carried a lot of guilt. Guilt about how easy it was to create magnetic energy with a man who was already in a relationship. Guilt that every time I pursued a man, there were always other women involved, and I didn't care about that as I should have. Guilt about the temptation to escalate relationships too quickly in search of validation.

Intimacy for me was constantly associated with crossing the line. When I was married, there was some sense of security because I had a wedding ring on. I felt safer knowing I could further disassociate with the seductress title I carried. I would purposefully flash my wedding ring, like a shield.

Once I went through my second divorce, this fear of everyone seeing me as the seductress came rushing back to me. *Now that most of my friends are married, would they assume just because I was single that I'd want their husbands? Is that branded on me as I walk around? Can I be trusted? Can I be alone with men and not create an air of sexual electricity or give them the wrong sign?*

Even if I was just talking to a man in a crowded room, it would trigger guilt and shame and paranoia that I am causing a man to assume the wrong thing about me. Since I had a history of not setting boundaries or saying no or being ethical at all, I tensed up. So not only did I stop smiling, but I stopped making eye contact with men. Every time I encountered one, I'd put up my guard. I didn't want to allow an intimate opportunity to open up.

In time, I became good at deflecting everyone, not just men. And it forced me to redefine what intimacy really means.

Restricting intimacy to sexual relations only means losing the true purpose that the word serves, which is real human connection. Intimacy means truly getting to know people through pure curiosity, without judgment, surpassing the surface, and creating a dynamic that allows that to breathe.

For a long time, I was caught in a cycle where I felt I was recognized by my name, job title, and perhaps a few other widely-known details, but not deeply known by many. Quite the opposite, actually, most of my relationships felt transactional at best. I didn't like that so many people were in my life for the titles I held. The moment those titles had an expiration date, the relationships seemed to as well. If I'd been asked, "Who truly knows you on the most intimate level?" I'd have stumbled over a response.

When I was younger, and begging to be seen and heard and understood, I didn't want a surface level acknowledgment. The intimacy I craved was for someone to truly understand me at the core of who I was, accept me for that, and still love me. And I wanted to reciprocate it, creating an equal give and receive. I was misguided in how I searched for it among men, but I'm able to see what I *really* wanted all along.

Now, I wholeheartedly believe that men and women can be friends, even when they are married, with the proper set boundaries and understanding. I know some people will disagree due to the stigma surrounding intimacy between sexes. However, I fully believe we need both masculinity and femininity balanced in the people we surround ourselves with. As women, we cannot expect for the only masculinity in our lives to come from our husbands, and then be surrounded by nothing but female friends. We cannot limit ourselves to what we are able to learn from intimate conversations with other people based solely on the sex that they are. Just like we shouldn't limit those conversations to people of a certain race, religion, or age. We are here to learn from everyone.

One of my gifts is creating an environment where people feel comfortable sharing and being open. I've always been able to provide that for men as well as women, and I don't want to turn away anyone by assuming that it will always turn sexual, especially when it comes to hearing their stories.

One of my favorite parts about being at the coffee shop is that I don't have to worry others may be concerned that I have ill intentions. Since day one, I have shown up as who I am today, with no remnants of my past, and my integrity locked in. I can have long conversations with women, men, with anyone, and they can go as deep as they're carried, and remain pure through and through.

Now that I feel comfortable having those types of conversations there, I'm confident they can happen elsewhere and maintain the same integrity.

It is unique finding people who are willing to get intimate, to share who they are, where they've been, what they've experienced, but I believe there is a shift happening in our society where it is becoming more common. Connecting with people on those levels creates deeper relationships. Depth in relationships allows people to wade through the muck of life and reveal the goodness and layers of their true identity. It's what strengthens us as a society because it prevents people from walking around unseen and unloved. It helps people feel more aligned with their purpose in this world.

When we repeat our personal stories time and again in comfortably intimate conversations, we become stronger in who we are. And when we share our stories with others, we can and will inspire them to do the same.

A beautiful cycle is formed.

I do a lot of writing from the coffee shop. It's the first time I don't mind interruptions in my writing as people stop by to talk because I know those interruptions are going to fill up my tank as much as my writing does. Those conversations and relationships are truly the essence of life. They're filled with hugs that last, and not surface chats, but ones that get to the truth of what we're experiencing in life. All around me people are diving deep into conversations that go for hours at a time. They're reading together and praying over each other. They're crying and laughing with each other. They're feeling safe to be who they were made to be. That is true intimacy.

I've finally become comfortable getting close to people again, trusting that it won't take a less-than-desired turn. It took a very long time to get here. I had to let go of the former stories I once believed. I really love people and want to know them for no other reason than to know them and show them they're loved. Before, I was constantly seeking to fill a void where I should have felt love and took it in any form I could. I regularly defaulted to anything sexual because I knew it was effective for a temporary fill.

Now, I'm not operating from a place of lack or seeking validation. I feel fulfilled through my relationship with Christ, with my kids, with my family, with my surrounding community. I know I have real love around me, and that means being accepted and loved even when I may have issues. Even though there may now seem to be a new reason for me to hold back, I refuse to let this smell paranoia be another reason to miss out on intimate moments with others.

Intimacy is something we all crave as humans. When we find it in the form of a safe community, as I've just found recently, it becomes obvious that we weren't meant for anything less.

rich, not broke

DURING ONE OF THE DARKEST PERIODS OF MY LIFE, I GOT a lot of comments saying, "Wow, I've seen your posts on social media, and you must be doing really well!" Prosperity in my business and life was being assumed based on my passionate social posts about writing and celebrating our clients.

I would just shake my head. *If only you knew there was $250,000 worth of debt over my head, and I am doubting every ounce of my existence.*

It was bad.

How did I get there?

Great question. How do we get anywhere in life? A bunch of tiny decisions that all led to one outcome.

My first couple of years in business, we did very well. We grew rapidly and I had a team in place. I spent a sickening amount of money on courses and mastermind programs to level-up my business and mindset. The experiences were good and I learned a lot, but constantly learning and implementing new strategies was exhausting because it never felt like I was doing enough, even though I was working nonstop.

Being in these programs with so many high-level entrepreneurs also shifted my focus from just being happy that I was getting to use my gifts to help others, to being more focused on revenue *only* and keeping up with the expectations of my peers. That was not a good pivot to make, and I know in hindsight, that energetic shift was detrimental.

The entrepreneurial world is heavily occupied by "spiritual junkies"; people who speak of God (or their version of God) in more universally-accepted and non-religious terms like the Universe or Higher Self or Source, among others. Immediately, I was informed of manifestation practices and crystals and all the things that are supposed to help me be successful. I was told we have all the power within us to change our lives and all we have to do is think the right thoughts. Suddenly, everything felt like, *Of course! I have full control! I can make anything happen that I want to happen!* It was like having God-like abilities.

One of the first big business connections I made was with a girl who had such an energetic light and heart of gold. She had seen me in some group on Facebook, and thought I'd be a perfect partner for a new organization of Energy Healers since so many wanted to write a book. I had no clue what that was so I had to learn a lot about it. The Healers were trained in the Emotion Code and other modalities, using their own bodies to heal people who needed it. I had my first energy healing session and immediately felt lighter and noticed a significant change within me. My exposure with these Energy Healers kickstarted my understanding of energy and vibrations, and how they affect us every single day.

The more involved I got with non-Christian spirituality, the more I doubted Christ and the God I went to church and Christian universities learning about. Suddenly, I was surrounded by non-religious people who made things *happen* in their lives. They were being proactive and taking charge. At the time, I believed the Church focused on sitting back and waiting on God, so as a dreamer and a doer, taking more control over my life was appealing.

As I started going down the spirituality path, the Bible became a patriarchal tool of control in my eyes and the story of Jesus became just another fictional tale.

This shift in my faith happened around the same time the divorce was decided. The moment we said we were going to get divorced, the business went from growing rapidly to suddenly drying up. It was almost overnight. I thought it was all temporary, but as month after month went by, I started believing that it was God punishing me for getting divorced. I believed I was being cast off for being a bad person and sinning. He finally had enough of all my stupid choices.

About two months afterward, I heard God very clearly say, "Shut down Burning Soul Press." The voice scared me and I was appalled—*there's no way that could have been God!* That's what I tried to convince myself, at least. Yes, we were down to a trickle of clients and income, but I knew it was just a temporary bump in the road. The clients coming in were absolutely amazing, and we were doing good in this world! *Why would God say to shut down a good thing?* Also, what else was I supposed to do for money as I became a single mom? And what was I supposed to do in life? This company I built was *everything* to me!

I ignored the voice, so in the meantime, I worked harder to keep control of the company and to keep God from taking it away.

The revenue dip felt temporary at the moment. A client would *almost* sign a significant contract but then have something else pop up so they'd have to push it off another month. *Okay, I'll take out a loan, it'll get repaid once the client pays, no problem.* Well, that happened again, and again, and again.

It started with opening a business credit card. Those are good to have anyway, but I didn't need it. We were operating in the green and doing fine. From there, it seemed the debt snowballed. From extending credit card amounts (both personal and business), to maxing them out, to opening lines of credit, to taking out business and personal loans, to cashing out my 401k and eating the penalties... it just kept adding up.

I charged premium prices for things like my ghostwriting services, but despite the hundreds of hours I'd pour into those projects, there'd be less than 10% that came into my pocket at the end of it all. The rest went into the business and payroll because I didn't have it set up the way I should have.

I held onto hope of *what was supposed to be* other than what actually was and was convinced it was going to all turn around again.

Then we had a round of a lot of things that just went bad. From bad partnerships to bad client choices (a few we shouldn't have taken on but did just to keep revenue coming in) to bad accountant and bookkeeper situations to just bad decisions from me as the CEO, which is what it mostly boils down to at the end. Those situations burned through a lot of money.

Eventually, the dire money situation forced me to let all my employees go—well, almost everyone. I had one person in particular who was my "everything" person. The yin to my yang. The perfect balance. One of the hardest parts about being an entrepreneur in the beginning is being a solopreneur, one that takes on everything and does everything. When this employee came on, it was clear she could learn as quickly as I did but also had the enthusiasm to take on new projects while also doing a great job.

I didn't want to be in a position to lose her; where she had to end up going someplace else while I was struggling and couldn't come back. I fought for her the most, like I'd fight for a once-in-a-lifetime relationship of any sort. The thing was, she was also my highest paid employee with health benefits, which meant a *lot* of additional fees to maintain salary and benefits.

Eventually, I ended up with $180,000 of high-interest debt (which as we all know, ends up being much more with interest month after month), and $70,000 of my own money being poured back into the business with nothing else to spare.

I dug a hole so deep that even though it felt like rock bottom, there was now high interest accumulating on top of the debt, so the hole kept getting deeper and deeper, month after month. It felt like there was no getting back up.

So much so, I'd be on the floor in the fetal position, crying out for help, with so much embarrassment and regret that I found myself there again. I had already made a promise to God that I wouldn't return to debt again like my past mistakes, and yet it went so much deeper than it ever had before. By *a lot*.

It got to the point that I was selling any physical item I had just to pay for food and other things. Money, or a lack of money, was all I could think about, creating constant heart palpitations. I grew tense with the kids and everyone else in my life because it's all I could think about.

One night, I woke up in the middle of a restless sleep and felt like I was choking on sand. All I could hear on repeat was, *I'm all dried up. I'm all dried up.* I couldn't stop choking.

I've always had a confusing relationship with money, thinking of it as more evil than good. Only in the past few years have I learned that money is neutral: it's what is done with it that makes it good or bad.

We didn't have a lot of money growing up and I saw my parents work hard to provide us with what we needed. I inherited thoughts that money was hard to come by and hard to make. I was the first to go to college and we had no wisdom about financial aid, so the private Christian universities I went to for both my undergraduate and graduate degrees paid in full by student loans were stupid decisions.

Then talk about the million times I've moved and have sold my things just to buy brand-new things, usually on a credit card because I rarely had cash. It's almost like anytime I had money, I had to get rid of it.

I have the mindset to give money and things away in a heartbeat. It's hard for me to have cash on hand without putting all of it in the tip jar at my favorite coffee shop or giving it to a homeless person on the street. If someone needed a couch, I'd say, "Come get mine, and I'll sit on boxes for a while!" I *love* giving things away.

But I learned that I can't give it all away, live on a credit card, and go into debt. Also, I can't always pay others and never pay myself, especially in my business. That's the way I tend to operate, though. Or used to. I had many lessons that God wanted me to learn during this time...

Another lesson that was becoming obvious was that I had too much of my identity wrapped up into Burning Soul Press. The mere idea of letting the company go shredded my ego. I also had too much dependency on other people guiding me on what I should be doing and how I was supposed to do it through all these crazy mastermind programs instead of trusting that God already gave me exactly what I needed to go where He was calling me to go.

Unfortunately, it got much worse before it got better.

This whole time, I was questioning where God was when I needed Him most. *And did I actually need Him?* According to what other people were saying, I could do all these things on my own. I was witnessing these super-spiritual people making things happen without God. It was appealing, since it's all about the endless things that we *can* do with no limitations except ourselves.

My spirituality crisis (and conscience crisis) forced me to push pause on the automatic beliefs that had been present for all my life. In one of the most difficult processes I've gone through, I started questioning *everything*, including why I believe the things that I do and why I do the things I do.

The process felt like I was burning down the pillars that once held me up, and the flames almost took me down for good. I had to then sort through the ashes to rebuild. I had to discover what was true to me, and not just adopted from, or influenced by, the people around me. There were months that I walked around detached to everything as I rebuilt my values and belief system. I felt half-dead.

It was through that deconstruction period when I started seeing holes in the spiritual perspective I had recently assumed. I saw how many of these practices and beliefs confused people at the core of their identities, leaving them spinning around in circles half the time. This ideology wasn't truly guiding them—or me—in the right direction; they were distractions from the truth.

Without any pillars of belief, as life crashed down around me, I fought suicidal thoughts again. Depression would come over me for days at a time. I thought I was a bad mom for putting my kids so at risk because of a "stupid dream." I thought I was having mini heart attacks at different points when my arm would go numb and my heart literally ached and I could barely breathe. I was receiving calls from collection agencies nearly thirty times a day. My credit score dropped tremendously.

I really wondered if I was indeed delusional, because I had held onto so much hope for so long for things to change. Sometimes, I thought I was just purely mentally insane.

I considered having to do quick-money things like an OnlyFans account or other ways that sell sex. Feeling so helpless was causing other past versions of myself to come up with thoughts like, *This is all you're good for anyway. Get back to it.*

There was no anchor this time, nothing to hold on to, feeling like there was no God close by because He was done with me. I felt hopeless, and like there was no way to come out of the darkness I was in. I felt like I ruined my life.

God was working in me at that time, though, even when I couldn't see it. He was sending me people who were helping to guide me back through simple conversations that I couldn't stop thinking about, and through the delivery of what I needed when I needed it that only God would have known. God had saved me hundreds of times, from car accidents to the suicidal attempts and a million moments in between. And here He was, still chasing me even after I'd turned my back on Him.

Although this whole period of being broken down to my core lasted two long years, me denying God and completely stepping away from my faith was only eight months of it. But one day, I was in my kitchen, and I suddenly fell to my knees out of the blue. It was as though the real truth hit me *hard*, and there was no more denying it. My God was never punishing me. He was teaching me. He was refining me. He was calling me into the role He wants me to be in but in no way was I actually prepared until I went through the two year journey that I did. He was loving me through it all. I declared Christ as my Savior for the second time in my life, except this time was different from when I was sixteen. There was nothing pretty about this conversion. This was grit, drowning in tears, being on the edge of ending my life again, and knowing that Him and I really wrestled this time, and it was, strangely, the exact thing I needed.

My relationship with Him this time around is different, my focus is on the Kingdom and not just what's happening in my day. I'm grateful I had that exposure to a different way of believing because it helped me understand the true power God has and the extent of the gifts He gives His people. My previous understanding of Him had too many restrictions on who He is and how He works through us, so it kept me within a strict set of limitations as well.

One of His gifts to me during this time came in the form of the most wonderful people who provided for me and my boys through food and household items and money when times were tough, even though they had no clue of the need that existed. They just listened to what God had told them. God showed He was there for me, even though I was (temporarily) sure He abandoned me.

I just had to learn a few lessons first. God needed to break me down a little bit and teach me that He is the only true Source, and sometimes that means sitting back and letting Him operate... which is *hard*. I'm a visionary and a dreamer, but I'm also very much a doer. I like to go after things and make them happen. I had to have my ego broken and bruised because I had to admit that *Yes, I need help.* And *No, I'm not this hugely successful entrepreneur who has it all together despite everything everyone assumes when they see me, and that's okay.* Because it wasn't ever supposed to be about the money; it was supposed to be about the work that was happening to bring light into this world, and I lost focus.

I learned there are so many beautiful lessons in the pain, waiting, and transition periods. All those bad moments I mentioned turned into the greatest learning opportunities. These are the periods I hate the most, until I'm on the other side and can say, "Look at what I learned in that time. Look at what God is doing."

I had to eventually tell that employee I fought so hard for that I thought it was the end. She worked part-time to help out with a few projects we had going on still and I was paying her out of whatever physical items I could sell or a few dollars that would trickle in from client work. At one point, I was five paychecks behind on paying her. Yet, she still stuck by my side. She was as loyal to me as I was to her, and that's a rare find.

The thing about being broke is that when everything gets stripped away, it allows us to become okay with less, okay with everything being gone. It doesn't feel great, but we learn how to survive, and we learn to see the people and things that really matter.

It's also one of the most confusing elements when sharing this story. In one moment, I was crying, hopeless, questioning everything, fighting dark thoughts, beating myself up for mistakes I made and wishing I had the knowledge that I have now.

But in the next moment, I was happy, not thinking about the looming debt, helping people write their stories, writing stories for others, writing my own books.

And it's how I started recognizing how rich I felt despite what my bank account or circumstances may otherwise show. It's why people see my social media posts and think I'm doing so well. Because I am indeed *rich*. I am rich because I discovered what I love doing in this world above all else. I've recognized my gifts, how I can help others, how I can contribute to this world, how I can help turn crappy things into something good. I recognized the people I don't want to live this life without and how I'm surrounded with more of them than I once thought.

Most of all, it got me to see that all the riches I crave already exist in He who made me.

Sometimes I wonder if that was the purpose of it all. To wake me up to how I was so focused on my own life, especially as I dove into non-religious spirituality, and get me refocused on the Kingdom and my contribution.

We do our best to operate in every present moment, but we don't truly know if what we're doing is the right or wrong thing until later, when we've had a chance to process it, when we've had a chance to reflect. I know the mistakes I've made in the past led me to where I am. I assume I've learned and that I won't ever repeat them again. I also assume some character development has happened as a result, because how could it not?

But I won't know for sure until I'm trusted with the treasures of my efforts again, with the harvest. Once I prove what I've learned and that I'm setting out to do things differently this time around, that's when I'll know for sure, and it'll be worth a celebration.

No matter what, I know God is walking with me as I fail and learn and grow on repeat, and that is the best and richest form of security I could ever have.

protected, not rejected

I'VE EXPERIENCED A LOT OF LOSS, BUT NOT IN THE WAYS most expect. Mostly in the form of relationships that ended by choice, not by death. When I'm kicked out of someone's life by choice, it feels like a rejection of who I am. Over and over again. It goes back to the feeling that the love that comes into my life is conditional—if I behave right, if I'm who they want me to be, if I do everything they expect of me, then I will be accepted, not rejected.

The person ironically responsible for planting the seed to write my memoir is my ex-mother-in-law. She was always incredibly supportive of my company. She read and bought every book we published, even if she wasn't a fan of the genre. We stood in our kitchen in Illinois during a visit in the midst of one of the most stressful times in my marriage with her son. She made the comment that I should write a memoir, without having any clue how much hurt I was experiencing from the marriage, or how much that would play a role in who I came to be as I wrote this memoir. At the time, writing a memoir wasn't on my mind, but she spoke the words that inspired this book.

It's interesting how much has changed since that moment. Not only the birth of this memoir, but also the divorce, a move from Illinois to Tennessee, how much pain and bitterness I've let go, and the growth in myself and life as a whole since. That was only four short years ago, and a testament to how much can truly change in such a brief snapshot of life.

One of the promises I made in the divorce, to myself and my kids, was to build up the family unit. I wanted us to remain close so they'd be surrounded by an extra big family who loves them. I dreamt of Christmases together, big birthday celebrations together, vacations together. I wanted that *so* badly. Maybe that's a little too crazy, but I still believed we could make this be anything we wanted it to look like and it could buck all the expectations of what anyone ever assumes a divorce needs to be. Because I loved his family like I love him and that seemed enough.

For the first couple of years, I was intentional to still wish his family members "happy birthday," to communicate and share updates about the boys with them, to still show love, especially to his mom who I still love and adore to this day. Birthdays in particular are meaningful to me, because they're the one day that people need to be celebrated—we're still on this planet and living and we deserve a special day once per year!

When my birthday would roll around, it was silent from his family. I was hurt and at the end of the night, I'd be sad, despite all the other friends, family, and random people saying happy birthday and pouring love into me. As dramatic as it may be, it was as though that one day each year told me everything I needed to know about how they feel about me; I was just in the family because of marriage but not cared for outside of that. It was hard for me to understand that just because a divorce took place, that it meant the love for each other had to end, too. My parents still wanted to talk to my ex-husband and still considered him family, so I couldn't fathom how his family wouldn't still consider *me* family. Their response was the standard way most people handle divorces, so I can't blame them.

Rejection shows up in tiny ways as much as it does in obvious ways. It happens when it feels like our security in *something* is suddenly threatened, whether love or acceptance. When the expectations we set are suddenly shattered. When we feel like reciprocity isn't equal. When someone chooses to go when we thought they'd be a permanent staple.

A few years ago, I lost my best friend of 22 years because of a choice she made. She let our friendship go seemingly because of guilt and a lack of self-worth. We had been through life together for years and years, there when no one else was. She was the one person who I could consistently be myself with, and although that was a novelty, I also learned it's something to be cautious about. We found comfort in showcasing the worst sides of ourselves, and not the best. It's nice feeling loved and accepted in our ugliest states, but it's unhealthy when we're not being the best of who we are as well.

Toward the end of our friendship, that became more and more clear. She was coming to me to share all the details about how she was cheating on her boyfriend with someone she loved. The one she was cheating with knew about her boyfriend; her boyfriend (who was an incredibly nice guy) had no clue.

I became her sounding board, and I approached it as though I was helping her sort through this. I thought I'd help her fix things, so she could move on. When she wanted to use my place and our hang out as a time to also invite and spend time with this man she was cheating with, that's when I spoke up. I told her how wrong it was to keep this going for so long and encouraged her to operate from a place of truth instead, to break up with her boyfriend until she could sort everything out.

When she refused to do so, I told her I couldn't continue to listen to her cheating escapades. I'd be there for all other parts of her life, but I couldn't stand by while she hurt herself by putting herself in this situation and hurt everyone else involved.

She didn't even give me the courtesy of speaking her mind to me. She just blocked me. In all forms—phone number, email, social media.

Twenty-two years of friendship that I poured into, and she ended it all over a disagreement about her cheating. All the snort-level laughter we shared, all the tears we cried, all the thousands of hours of phone calls and text messages, and being there for each other when no one else seemed to be—*over*.

Truthfully, that cut deeper than either of my marriages ending. I thought about her every single day for two years afterward, and frequently for some time after that. To this day, out of curiosity, I still pull her up on social media, curious if she ever went as far as to unblock me.

Nope, still blocked.

I was talking to someone about this who had also lost her best friend in a similar manner. And she asked, "Do you still think of her almost all the time?" And it was a resounding yes for both of us. I haven't had a romantic relationship linger for that long, but a friendship ending is a harder pill to swallow. Especially when I thought she'd be there until the end of time. We used to joke about growing old together and how much fun and laughter we would have. There was a commitment, a loyalty, a knowing that even after every other relationship ended, we'd have each other.

However, I was proud that I established a boundary with her, something I wouldn't be a part of; there were just consequences as a result, and that's okay.

God's Best has been ringing in my ears lately. I've allowed myself to settle for much less than that in the past. When we settle for less than the bar that was established for us time and time again, what we confirm to ourselves is that we are less than what we truly desire.

It's so easy to get down on ourselves and wonder, *Was I not worthy of what I thought was something really amazing?* When in fact, perhaps it just wasn't good enough for *us*. The stories we tell ourselves scream that we're not good enough, but things that happen for us have to be screened by Him. Especially once we hold ourselves to the standard that we deserve. *Do I really want my best friend to be one that I can't be my best with in having higher standards for myself, for her, and for this life?* Absolutely not. So why hold on so strongly to something that proved it definitely is not what I'm truly deserving of?

This concept completely shifted how I started viewing dating as well. Dating on the brink of turning forty is more challenging, because everyone is bringing baggage and various levels of trauma to the relationship that have to be sorted through. However, I recently met a man who set a whole new standard for me, the bar higher than it's ever been before. I would have thought he was God's best for me, based on what he was saying and how he lived his life. However, God knew the truth. The man left and my first thought was, *What did I do wrong? What was it about me that wasn't good enough for him? What do I need to fix about myself to make myself better for him?*

On a morning walk, still feeling sad and reflecting on this, I watched the sky turn colors. The spread-out rainbow, the beauty, the way the light was causing me to look up instead of watching the sidewalk. When I looked into the light, pulling myself out of this internal "woe is me" dialogue, I felt a sense of calmness, and in part, relief. Calm because the promises that I'm worthy of God's best didn't change. That still held true. Nothing circumstantial changed that promise. Relief because it's not on me to figure out what went wrong or try to repair something that may not even need repaired (meaning me, or the relationship). I could let go and trust that if this wasn't the best, the best is yet to come, and it's a glimpse of how good things could really be.

The truth is that this wasn't another form of rejection as I'd thought; it was God's call for the best He has for me and my chance to accept it. God knows the man who set the bar, He knows the man who is the best for me, and He knows my heart and He's protecting me. As long as I keep my eyes on Him, the best will come.

That shift in perspective allows me to work less toward something that feels like a big desire. Don't get me wrong, I'll work at a relationship once it's here, but in the meantime, I don't have to take on *all* the effort to bring it into my life. The deal I have with God is that, for once, I'm letting go of control and trusting He will bring the right man into my life. This may not be the same for everyone, but my past was dictated by my constant search for the next man who would soon hurt me. I never sat back and waited for the right one. It's a pattern I've had to learn to break, which is why I'm waiting on Him from here on, because I only want what's best.

It is so much easier to breathe in relationships once we let go of the fear of rejection; when we actually accept that we're enough, even when we're still a work in progress; when we realize that there's a God who is watching out for us, wanting to deliver the best He has for us, and all we have to do is accept it.

Ease suddenly ripples through my body at the thought... *I am protected from the things that are not meant for me.*

We may want to hang on to certain people forever, but if they want to go, we need to let them. It doesn't mean we need to replace the love in our hearts for them; we just don't need to stop life and wait by the door for their return. Consider it a time to celebrate what we learned from their time in our life, and the excitement of what could be even better soon coming in.

People sow what they think they're worth, and I'm only going to harvest the best of the best from here on out.

restored, not destroyed

I WAS GOING THROUGH SOME PAPERWORK, TRYING TO find records for my dogs, and through it, I discovered all the papers documenting bits of my life I wasn't proud of.

Loans for ridiculously high amounts that I struggled to pay off, starting from the time I was in college and got sucked into private school loans followed by credit cards, and the list went on.

Divorce paperwork for two dissolved marriages in two different states.

A deed in lieu of foreclosure for my first house purchase.

Receipts for an insane number of bad purchases.

Adoption paperwork for cats and dogs that I later gave up.

Bills, bills, bills.

As I went through it, I felt myself deflate. I heard that dark voice say about a hundred times, "Look at how badly you've screwed up your life. You destroyed all the good things you had. You destroyed your life."

The voice was soon screaming at me.

I had to shut it down fast. I closed the box with all the paperwork, and got away from it.

Here I am, writing this book about reframing our narratives and feeling the happiest I have in a long time, and I open up a box that reflected every poor decision I've ever made (and there have been a lot!) and *whoooosh!* I was knocked down a peg, reminded of how much of a failure and disappointment I spent years believing I was.

When I started writing this memoir, it was a lot darker than it is today. I knew I felt called to share my story, but I also knew I was very much *in* my story. I didn't want to let that stop me, though, because I also knew I couldn't write it once I was dead.

I decided to keep some pieces of the darkness. I've changed since then, so much that I have a slight distaste for some of the language used. Nonetheless, here is one original piece that probably could have been a journal entry:

2020 was a high in my life despite the shit of the world.
2021 was an "oh fuck" period and the shit of the world aided it.
2022 was an "I have nothing left" period and the shit of the world didn't matter.

As I write this right now, it's a few days away to September 2022. This year has been filled with highs as well as lows. The highs were high and the lows were really fucking low.
As I write this, I'm flat broke.

Worse than flat broke.

Like in the red and maxed out on every credit card. Interest piling up in thousands of dollars per month because I'm so maxed out.
And revenue barely trickling in.
I haven't been able to pay myself for the last four pay periods.
I've scrambled to pay my employees.

We're days away from the end of the month, and I have no way to pay my rent outside of the final credit card... and no way to pay the $15,000 in bills due in a few days.
It's weird that it feels like there's no one who wants to work with us

anymore. We launched a program that isn't taking off like I hoped it would. Ad money is being spent but nothing landing.
I just don't get it.

Then my mom texted today to tell me that she took me off their will as the main executor. She said it was due to distance with me now living in Tennessee.
But all I felt was rejection.

Something else being taken away. Something else that makes me feel unwanted. Me not being good enough. Me fucking everything up.

My mind spiraled and the tears flowed.
I know there's a depressive part of my spirit that still attacks. It comes up in moments like these.
But I try to stay optimistic... I fight for what I want... and then it just feels like it all crashes down around me.
I'm at the point that I don't know what to do anymore. Almost like this "all hope is lost" point.

Now, in a fiction story, this is when things start turning around. When the hero has reached rock bottom and there doesn't seem to be any way out of the dire situation...then BAM! Opportunity arises. Cue the betterment of life to come.

There are also points when the hero thinks it's bad and it gets worse.

Fuck I hope that's not where I'm at.

I've been seeing butterflies like crazy lately. Enough for me to ask if there's a purpose behind them. So I looked up the symbolism of butterflies. They stand for growth, rebirth, transformation... all things I can relate to and have been experiencing and going through lately.

They also stand for afterlife, and sometimes I wonder if I'm going to

die soon. But what a shitty way to go out—with debt and unfulfilled dreams.
I had a weird thought strike me last week... something about how I'm dying in September.
It's the same voice that spoke to me years ago when I thought for sure I wouldn't live past thirty-two.
I'm not sure where it's coming from.
But this is not the way I want to go out.

I just feel like I went from living my passion to being back on a damn hamster wheel. Going around and around, struggling, pulling, sinking in quicksand...
I can't recall a time I've ever felt so hopeless.
Everything shifted when I made the declaration about my divorce.
It was like revenue plummeted and I haven't been able to gain traction since.
Granted I made a lot of bad decisions in-between, but it always feels like the catalyst, the moment I go back to and blame.
And I don't know why I do that.

I have to let it go. Let go of the idea that that one decision led to this. Let go of the idea that no one wants me, that no one wants to work with me, that this was never something more than what it was.
I have to let go of the nagging feeling that I'm useless. Out of alignment. Pointless.

I'm just praying for a miracle. I feel like I've been taking action after action after action trying to drum something up... and now all I can do is just pray.
Pray for a change. I know I can live a life better than this... I know there's something I'm supposed to learn in this... but God I don't want to keep going through this. Please help me out of this.

I want to write, I want to help others, I want a life of abundance, I want to make a difference. I want to spend time with my kids. I want to invest in things that matter. I want to leave behind a legacy. I want to do so much more than what I'm doing now.

There's giving up.
And there's giving up the things that don't serve you.
There's a difference.
Many times I thought about giving up. Things weren't working. Things were too hard. My emotions were spiraling. I refused to give up on business because I can't imagine doing anything else. I knew the hardships were building my character. I was getting tougher, even when I felt weak in the moment. I was learning lessons that I refused to learn before.

I was also taking note of patterns that were occurring. Ones completely within my control, whether it be the thoughts I think or the people I attract and allowed to come into my sphere, whether it was the moments I refused to see people for who they were, believing in who they could be instead.
So I took note, and I learned.

I gave up alcohol for multiple reasons.
The last time I drank, I drank too much where I was out the next day. All day. On the floor, throwing up.
I also used alcohol to justify my actions. Actions that I would take if I was bold enough any other time but at least if I got embarrassed or if something happened that I didn't want to happen, I could blame it on drinking. It's always easier to blame something else than ourselves.

The problem with alcohol that I loved is that there was a sweet spot in those moments between just starting to drink, and drinking too much, where I was able to find that my brain finally connected to my mouth. Where the rapid-fire, Gilmore Girls-style talking could come out easily, my mouth keeping up with my thoughts, saying what I wanted instead of the continual disconnect that seemed to take place. That was the most addictive part of drinking for me.

But the fact that I was using it as a justification for the actions I wanted to take and the words I wanted to speak, was the problem. It was becoming a crutch.
It was also becoming the thing I leaned on when I was with guys. The last few men I slept with, alcohol was involved, and I just remember blacking out for most of the sex.
Alcohol wasn't serving me.
Strangely, once I let alcohol go, I let the men who should have never been worth my time go, too.

Many times, the only way to move forward is by letting things go. Maybe they were things that were good for one season of life but they no longer serve where we want to go. Whether people, old beliefs, habits, or even our goals. When we keep everything the same, we stay stagnant. But when we're willing to let everything go, we have a chance to grow. Sometimes it just has to feel like it's being taken away without our consent to get to that point. Like relationships, friends, and even my business.

The crazy part of it all? With all the darkness I had been through, I actually thought, "Yep, I'd go through it again just to know what I know today. Just to be so much more wrapped up in God as I am today."

And even in the times that it feels like the world has completely stopped, that nothing is moving, that I'm in this deep hole with no hope whatsoever, if I go back to this idea of, "What am I supposed to learn from this?" It reminds me that I'm still learning, even when it feels like nothing around me is changing.

Things have changed quite a bit since this was written, and it's what I love about being able to write and reflect on old pieces. We're constantly evolving as long as we're learning as we move through this life.

This "new life," this second chance, was given to me to truly love myself, to love others, to put good into this world, and to turn shame into power. I have times when I feel somewhat invincible. I feel so strong mentally and emotionally that I feel like if hardships, challenges, emotional destruction tries to come my way, there is no way I will succumb. I've done the work, I've gathered the tools, I've learned how to protect myself.

But then there are times I'm suddenly on the ground, sobbing, feeling like the worst screw up.

What's important to recognize is that just because I've progressed and worked damn hard on myself throughout the years, it doesn't mean there won't be setbacks. I have to give myself grace.

It's particularly hard when it feels like the past keeps resurfacing. The things that I've come to terms with, or so it seems, and suddenly return, in my face like the ugly demons they are.

When those moments take over, it can be challenging to remind myself, *that person is no longer you.* It's not who I was made to be. It's not who I am today. It's not who I need to associate with anymore.

I am not destroyed. It is not the end of me. The times I've contemplated suicide in my life, wondering if I should just give up everything, if I'm worthless... it's not the end until it's the end. So, what am I fighting for in the meantime?

I am fighting for myself and what I'm meant to do for this world, because I've finally learned that's enough.

I have been restored because I trust in Christ and keep moving forward.

I have been restored because I choose to be.

Because even when I don't feel like my complete self, it is a choice that I can still make to turn my life around tomorrow. To honor the feelings that rise sharply and fiercely out of the blue.

Understanding and recognizing that I can feel destroyed in the moment, but it doesn't prevent me from being redeemed or restored.

It is a whirlwind to be broke beyond broke while simultaneously discovering such a strong love for people's stories and growing in my faith in Jesus. One of the best things that has come from it is that I've started to understand the concept of dying to myself daily and being receptive to what He has in store for me instead.

That's the thing about feeling like nothing is good and everything has gone to crap... it's easier to give up control because I succumb to the realization that everything I've tried to control in the past hasn't worked.

By allowing God to take over, some of the most beautiful moments have taken place. From money showing up in my account when I need it the most, to friends dropping off exactly what I need, to the most wonderful people surrounding me and praying over me. Somehow I'm working less, but making more, not just in my business, but in all areas of my life. His goodness is showing up everywhere.

He proved to me that I've always been in His hands, even when I couldn't see it. He's continued to provide time and again, showing I'm not alone, even in all the times I thought I was.

As of the publishing of this book, the debt I found myself in had shrunk by about 80% in a whopping three months' time. I heard the promise that my debts are as washed away as my sins are, and I knew that to be true. Because like I sinned in a time of darkness, I got into debt in a time of darkness. Coming out, falling to my knees again to acknowledge Christ as my Savior, learning so much of Him is in me, and me in Him, the debt is crushed. The darkness is crushed.

Christ has it all, and I surrender to Him.

I was watching someone at church one day who by physical standards, may not be the strongest person in the room. But when she is worshiping and standing in the presence of God, she is strong, glorious, beautiful. She is a powerful oak tree dancing freely and firmly in both the sun and the storms. I know a bit of her story and the unimaginable pain she had been through, but that's not what you see if you'd watched her worship. All anyone could see was someone who surrenders herself to God while harboring the strength to take down any goliath in her path. I couldn't take my eyes off of her and by watching her, *I* felt empowered.

When things get hard, I think back to that vision of someone who has learned to both surrender and fight at the same time.

It's all about *what* we're surrendering to and *what* we're fighting for that makes a difference in our lives. It may have taken the destruction of almost everything important to me in my process, but I came back to life restored with a sword and a warrior-like faith and a clear vision of what I'm here to do, no matter what blocks my way.

whole, not broken

SOMEONE TOLD ME RECENTLY THAT I REALLY NEED TO work on loving myself more.

I was pissed that they could say such a thing. I had spent the last two years of my life learning to love myself more. I love myself more now than I've ever loved myself before.

So what did they mean that I needed to love myself *more*?

Turns out I did. Turns out I was hanging onto a lot of limiting beliefs and baggage that I hadn't let go. Just two months before, I had thought about leaving this world.

I'd captured my journey up to 2022 in this book. It was fascinating to comb through it in late 2023 and prepare it for publishing. I've re-read the stories and thought, *I really held onto a lot of unnecessary crap for many years.*

Because I wasn't breathing fully, uncomfortable to be myself, I felt it in the weight I carried.

What I find interesting is it seems that the more self-aware a person is and expressive about it, the more someone will say that they are broken.

Yet the more quiet someone is about their life, people will assume that they have all their shit together.

When usually, it's quite the opposite.

When I stay quiet, it's because I'm trying to pull myself out of a hole I've slipped into. It's because I'm feeling hopeless. It's because I'm feeling unloved. It's because I'm falling apart.

When I'm expressive, it's because I've processed. I'm completely fascinated by the way we can have this rollercoaster type of experience in life, where one day, it feels like the end, but if we hold on just a little longer, we'll look back and say, "Holy shit, look who I've become now!"

I've been so open about my struggles because I want people to know they're not alone, but I'm also realizing how I sometimes establish a bond with people based on the negative stories in our lives. Sometimes I feel like it gives us things to talk about on a deeper level.

But I also sometimes wonder if we don't have those, what are we supposed to talk about? Can we really have a deep bond with someone if we only talk about the positive things that happened in our lives?

I think the truth is somewhere in the middle.

There is something that connects us on a spiritual level when it comes to *overcoming*. It's not just about struggling or the positive result once we're on the other side, it's about the journey to get there. Overcoming is about sharing the places where we once were and comparing them to where we are today; it's a mutual sense of excitement and being in awe of how we can move through life in this way. Even if we're not *currently* overcoming, we see ourselves in people's struggles and we see that it's possible to get to the other side. Hope and inspiration connects us.

I joked with my seventeen-year-old niece, that if she wants to learn about what *not* to do in life, she ought to come to me. I tend to teach first about what I did wrong before I start teaching on what I did right. Many times for me, it took the wrong moves to find the right ones.

There are several major turning points in my life, but two are more recent. One was when I had my boys and became a mom (with both of them, not just with one for all the lessons to completely sink in), and the other was starting Burning Soul Press. It's as though I lived multiple lifetimes in a short period between those two events because of all that happened, and all I've learned. I look back at a period where I was naive and without boundaries, at what I've been forced to learn through all the hardships, but how I grew a wiser soul as a result.

Mostly, I feel like a totally different person.

For so much of my life, I wanted people to love me, but how was I to demand anyone love me when I wasn't even loving myself? When I wasn't even sure of who I was because broken pieces were so scattered everywhere? How could I expect anyone to love me for me if I wasn't being myself? I was looking in all the wrong places for what I needed.

I had to let God work in my life, even though some of the situations weren't ideal, to rebuild me as a whole person, so I could fall in love with who I am.

When the boys were both in my womb, I would sit in a rocking chair and sing "Jesus, Lover of My Soul" over and over again. I don't know why that song would come to me, but it was the only one I could think to sing in those moments.

There was a time when Camden was three and Easton was five, and I had them in my arms before bedtime, and I just started singing it again, for the first time in three years. They both stayed motionless and completely silent the entire way through that song. Then both asked me to sing it again.

There was a part of them that could remember that song, even in the womb, and it brought them comfort.

Now we sing it most nights before bed, and they sing it with me. The joining of our three voices as we sing this song is one of the most special things I've experienced.

What's interesting is that before I started singing it to them while I was pregnant, the last time I had ever sung that song was twelve years earlier when I was twenty and finally put away the orange "Wow Worship" CD. I loved that CD from ages sixteen to twenty, immediately buying it after I was saved. However, if I had to pick a song that I would later sing in my future, "Jesus, Lover of My Soul" wouldn't have been my choice. There were others I sang far more often.

When I looked up the CD to reference it for this book, I noticed that the person who sang *that* song on *that* album was Darlene Zschech. This community that I found and fell in love with? It's HopeUC, the same global church led by Darlene and her husband. I didn't even know that until after attending services for three weeks, and now, only now after remembering that CD, do I see the full-circle connection.

God has brought all of my broken pieces back together and led me to exactly where I'm supposed to be today. I was being guided, even when I refused to follow the steps I was supposed to take. I was being listened to, even when I thought I was ignored. I was being loved, even when I pushed love away.

I don't see myself as a broken person anymore. I see myself as a masterpiece that tells a unique story. It's my story, and it's important, and even though it's not yet over, the more whole I become, the more at peace I feel for when that time may come.

Every night I have the kids, I kiss them goodnight and tell them how proud I am of them. They never ask, "Why are you proud, Mama?" But the reason I tell them every night is because I'm proud of who they are when their heads hit the bed at night. I'm proud that they prayed with me right before bed, making the time to talk to God, and that they made it through the day so that we were all here, together, at the end. I'll watch them, long after they have fallen asleep, thanking God for them.

Their existence in this world matters deeply to me, and I know they will matter to many others as they go through their lives. Every decision, every turn of events, every up and down, everything will matter, as will the lens they view their experiences through.

For as long as we're here in this world, every word and every action is making a difference, even in the moments they're going to feel broken. And as much as I want them to know that their lives matter, I want everyone else to know it as well. But it had to start with my recognition that my own life matters, too.

powerful, not ashamed

As I was preparing this memoir for publishing, I had a friend of mine who is in her fifties say, "I was shocked to see you were writing your memoir. You're too young. Isn't that for older people who have lived life?"

That mentality is not uncommon, and part of my calling is to erase this old way of thinking. I want people to realize how important every single one of our stories truly are, no matter where we are in life. We aren't guaranteed to live to a certain point, so how can we say we have to wait until a certain age before writing about our life? Who's to say a twenty-year-old hasn't had more life-altering revelations than a sixty-year-old? It's not about time spent in this world; it's about *how* that time is being spent and what you're learning as a result. That sharing of experiences and learning is what makes anybody's story important. All the other facts don't matter. Everyone is qualified simply by the experience of life they've had.

My experiences in my life have allowed me to empathize with more people, to understand them better, to give them more grace. I've had to give myself more grace as well. When I share things about my life, I always have a little bit of a worry that people are thinking, "Wait, how did it take you so long before you realized *that*?" Some people may have come to the conclusions I have much earlier than I did and there are people who are also much older than me who have yet to learn these things. We're all on different journeys, moving at different speeds, and all that matters is that we're learning.

And I love learning about what we're *all* learning. Which is why I love hearing people's stories so much.

Our life is one long, beautiful series of amazing stories. We get so addicted to TV shows or movies or book series, fascinated by other people and hooked to the continuation of "what happens next," but we miss out on being fascinated by our own stories.

As scary as it was to write this memoir, it was also fun to open up a bunch of old "boxes" and remember things I would have thought I'd never think about again. But with having a new perspective and lens on life, I let my curiosity take over, exploring every angle, including what I could see, what I felt, and what was probably *actually* happening. I became fascinated by my journey and how writing about that person I once was, even up to two years ago, felt like writing about a completely different human being.

Most of my fiction books are heavily influenced by the idea of second chances. Once we finally break out of old patterns, what can we do with our life when we're ready to live differently? I write about it because I rarely got things right the first time (or even the second time), but I love that life lets me try again.

I'll let you in on a little secret: I started this book originally *only* focused on all the shame I held, wanting to challenge myself to put every single shameful moment down on paper and force myself to face it. I wanted to be the brave soldier on the frontlines helping everyone else shake the unnecessary darkness in their lives, the things we aren't proud to share, but are still important elements of our journey and who we are today. "Undressing the Shame" was going to be the title. Even when I had that title, I had some sort of lingering concept behind the idea to break down the shame and rewrite the narrative.

But God was working in my life in significant ways. And the thing is, a book title, especially one that's about my life, hangs around forever. *Did I really want to permanently connect shame into my identity, even if it was an attempt to buck it? Aren't I more than that?*

I am absolutely more than the shame that tried to imprison me. Shame may have held one of the leading emotion roles in my life, but I've also converted it into power to help me connect with people and make a positive difference. It could have been a dark force but I chose to turn it into light because *the choice is ours.* So I wrote this book to expand not just on shame, but on other things that shaped who I am as well. Because ultimately it's all the stories that we tell ourselves that influence the choices we make each and every day.

One of my favorite parts about people writing their story is this: the more they capture those life stories and honor how the stories have all contributed to who they are today, the easier those stories are to tell to others. The more we share our stories, the more power we feel behind our voice as we tell them. The more power we can identify in the sharing of our stories, the more confident we can feel in our roles here, our purpose, and how we can truly make a difference. Suddenly, we're telling different kinds of stories that serve a *new* message.

I believe we get little nudges (or Golden Butterflies) for a reason. Yes, for ourselves, but also because we are connected in ways we have yet to know, to someone else who needed to hear or read exactly what we felt called to say or write. Ultimately, it's always our stories, above all else, that connect us and create the bonds that we build.

My favorite part about seeing our clients release their books is watching those hidden connections become visible; once strangers start telling the author that their story changed their lives. It's a beautiful ripple effect that continues throughout time because books get passed down from one set of hands to another, connecting people to each other, and to the author, through each exchange.

But it's important to note that it all starts with the author of that story accepting the nudge for the idea, then writing and finishing the message or book they felt called to share in the first place. If it never leaves their mind, heart, notebook, or computer, it never has a chance to impact the people who need it the most.

The inevitable evolution of self can be an excuse that holds a lot of people back from writing their story and sharing it as a memoir in the first place.

"What if I write my story and I'm no longer that same person?"
Then you're doing life exactly as intended.

Who I was when I started writing this book is different from who I was when I finished it.

That's a good sign.

I believe that every single book we read, if it's a good one, should alter us in some way. It should add value, even if it's just getting us to think for a moment from a completely different perspective. Some books can cause more significant change in us, some we may not even notice.

So why should an author writing the book expect anything other than to be changed, too?

Every single second of every single day has the ability to change us. We are making choices constantly. We are given new chances to pay attention to one thing that we may have ignored the day before; to study, to understand ourselves, other people, the world; to learn how to best work together, and to take care of one another.

If we're doing life right, we don't stop growing in *some* way.

Writing a memoir isn't our one-time chance to tell our story. It doesn't lock us into being that person forever since we should still be learning and evolving for as long as we're living. In fact, if we write one memoir, we can write another. It can be done in *so* many ways! These books are our personal monuments in our journeys, showing where we've been and how we became who we are as the end inevitably comes.

The best part about writing your own memoir? You can choose the theme of what you want to share and how much you want to share. I may have shared beyond a personal boundary you have for yourself, and that's okay. I couldn't write a book that had a theme of turning shame into power if I wasn't going to get into the depth of my most shameful moments.

There are many pieces of my life and parts of who I am, many of which I've shared already, that I can say I'm not proud of. They're not the most pleasant pieces to write about on a piece of paper and hand over for other people to read, judge, and criticize. They're not exactly the pieces I'm excited for my kids to know about someday. I also know I've done enough judging of it that no one else can sling any worse thoughts my way than what I've already done.

But I'm also *really* proud of who I am today and it took my entire journey to become this person.

This book will forever represent me and this time in my life, so I wanted it to be all the pieces of myself. The good, the ugly, the shameful, the growth. Because *all* the pieces contributed to who I have become today: a daughter of the King, a grateful mother, a passionate writer; and it's still not the end. My story may have shaped me, but I know what defines me, and that will produce a different story as I continue moving through this life.

The thing is, my shameful moments may be extreme for some people, and others won't bat an eye because their shameful moments aren't even in the realm of comparison. But for me, my shame stayed with me, preventing me from stepping into my true light, my true identity, my true gifts, my true purpose. It was only by identifying the stories I told myself, allowing me to uncover the heart of my shame, that I was able to take back control and find my inner power. Now, I don't slink away from shame; I face it. I can call it whatever I want, and shame doesn't have to be the name. It no longer owns me because I'm who I was made to be, and I'm proud of every single element that has helped me get here.

"For whatever is hidden is meant to be disclosed, and whatever is concealed is meant to be brought out into the open."

Mark 4:22

acknowledgments

To my favorite coffee shop and writing place, the beautiful 1819. A place that taught me how to feel comfortable being myself even in public with new people all around. I can be in the moment and not think about the future. I'm at peace. I'm inspired. I'm lost in conversations. I'm ready for more. It feels like a training ground for the bigger world. It's a very special place to me for many, many reasons and is where 80% of this book was written.

To my Hope UC family for teaching me so much in this pivotal time of writing my life story and inspiring me with all the conversations that gloriously interrupted my writing time. You're the community I never even knew I was dreaming about until I found you.

To my real family for helping me grow and be weird and make mistakes and always come back home in new versions of who I am, and loving me anyway. Especially in the last couple of years, I've become even more grateful for the roles you all have played. I know this memoir won't be easy to read for those who choose to take it on, but even in the ups and downs, you all have shaped who I am in beautiful ways. These days I appreciate being back home with you all more than ever and know there will always be laughter and fun— and the one place I can always easily nap.

To Allison, my right-hand woman, my editor, my safe space, my friend. You are the one who has had a first-account perspective of all the good and bad over the past three years. Thank you for not giving up on me, for staying committed to the vision I've had, and believing in me when others would have turned their back. You had every reason to walk away multiple times, and you stuck through it, even when working tirelessly and not receiving any pay for it, showing true love and loyalty like no one else. I couldn't have done any of this without you.

To Kellee, for jumping in and editing this book as well, always being willing to take on any new work I've done with gusto. You've always been one of my biggest supporters and loyal friends, and your encouragement and belief in me always has me in awe. Thank you for your endless love.

To my kids, Easton and Camden, the truest joys of my life. You are my continual teachers. I want nothing more than to be able to set the best example for you both. I want you to always be rooted in who you were made to be, to always love deeply like the love of Christ, to embrace your unique gifts and use them to better this world, and to stand strong because you know how loved you are for simply being you no matter what. The one thing I'll always be the most grateful for is you. Always. There are not enough words or paper for me to share how much I love you and how proud I am of you, but I hope you always feel it in every ounce of who you are.

And of course to God, who has been working miracles within me and in my life forever, but working especially hard the past few years. Thank you for making me be more than I ever realized I could be, and showing my true worth when I refuted it for so long. Thank you for rescuing me time and time again, protecting me, and never giving up on me. Thank you for working all the bad in my life to still serve your Good. Thank you for calling me to be a warrior for you and toughening me up to be a force that helps bring people to you.

May these words and stories reach the people they were meant to reach, in hopes of helping at least one, and inspire a few more stories to be shared with the world.

about the author

Lauren Eckhardt is an award-winning and best-selling author, ghostwriter, and book coach, and the CEO of Burning Soul Press. Her life purpose is helping people capture their life journey through a book, whether just for them, their family, or to share it with the world. She's also the mama to two little guys who are her why that drives her every day to create a better world through the stories that inspire and empower others, while bringing light to those who need them the most. Lauren lives in Nashville, Tennessee surrounded by many, many books.

www.LaurenEckhardtWrites.com
Follow Lauren: laureneckhardtwrites on IG & Facebook

 To see photographs of moments showcased in this memoir and to access mentioned playlists, podcasts, and more, scan the QR code to view all the exclusive supplemental material.

or go to LaurenEckhardtWrites.com/Memoir-Scenes

 facebook.com/laureneckhardtwrites
instagram.com/laureneckhardtwrites

also by lauren eckhardt

The Second Chance Spark Series
Women's Fiction

The Remedy Files
Young Adult Dystopian

Made in the USA
Middletown, DE
28 February 2024

50528095R00135